A

GIFT TO YOU

from the

COAST GUARD ACADEMY FOUNDATION

Roger M. Wilhelm

DECEMBER, 1973

EAGLE VENTURES

PUBLISHED BY
M. EVANS AND COMPANY, INC., NEW YORK
AND DISTRIBUTED IN ASSOCIATION WITH
J. B. LIPPINCOTT COMPANY,
PHILADELPHIA AND NEW YORK

EAGLE VENTURES

BY WILLIAM I. NORTON

Illustrations on pages 16, 24, 26, and 27 from *The History of American Sailing Ships* by Howard I. Chapelle, Copyright © 1935 by Howard I. Chapelle, by permission of W. W. Norton & Company, Inc.

Illustrations on pages 101 and 105 from *Eagle Seamanship: Square Rigger Sailing,* W. I. Norton (ed.), Copyright © 1969 by M. Evans & Company, Inc., by permission of the Coast Guard Academy Foundation, Inc.

COPYRIGHT © 1970 BY WILLIAM I. NORTON
ALL RIGHTS RESERVED UNDER INTERNATIONAL AND
PAN AMERICAN COPYRIGHT CONVENTIONS
LIBRARY OF CONGRESS CATALOG CARD NUMBER: 72–126390
MANUFACTURED IN THE UNITED STATES OF AMERICA
DESIGNED BY ELLEN HSIAO

CONTENTS

DEDICATION

*To the elite of American youth—
seafaring men with a high sense of
honor, loyalty and obedience; leaders
destined for greatness, strong in the resolve
to serve their country; men who will be
the champions of a new generation of
humanity—the future officers of the
United States Coast Guard.*

FOREWORD

"To me, the sea is a continual miracle," Walt Whitman wrote, "the fishes that swim—the rocks—the motion of the waves—the ships that have men in them.

"What stranger miracles are there?

"The way of a ship in the midst of the sea—the way of a ship . . . it is too wonderful for me."

Whaleships hunting the oceans and clippers that took men's breath away remain only in the rhymes of poets and in museums of modeled nostalgia. Even the longest memory has only a dim recollection of the last square-riggers to leave snug New England coves and head for Cape Horn. After all her centuries of service, the great sailing ship has gone her way.

Yet, men cannot bring themselves to abandon the adventure of sailing on the seas. Each in his own way, modern wanderers still go down to the sea seeking the freedom and challenge that waits beyond quiet harbors.

My challenge has been in skippering a variety of racing sail craft and in twice defending the prized *America*'s Cup.

Others have found fulfillment in a myriad of ways under sail—in club racing, in crewing on charter sail vessels, in leisure day-sailing and in cruising the oceans to exotic ports-of-call.

Still, we all share the traditional way of seafaring. As if we had dreamed ourselves back into that long-ago time when sail still spread its ancient beauty across the waters of the world, we delight in mastering the mariner's skills and in feeling a deck underfoot.

No matter how grand or how modest our craft, nor how daring or simple our course, the fact that we love to go to sea under sail makes each of us kin to Cape Horners of old and heir to the saltiest clipper captains.

This legacy of the great days of sail has been preserved for us in another way—in the handsome square-rigged training bark *Eagle,* sailed by the young men of the United States Coast Guard Academy. Through this fine ship every American can still sense the pride of all who sailed square-riggers and know the wonder of all who beheld them.

I have often encountered this lovely ship under full canvas, both of us sailing briskly off the shores of New England. And each time we've met, I've gained new inspiration and a deep sensation of belonging to our seafaring past.

Now such fleeting moments can be enjoyed again and

again. For here, in this book, the *Eagle*'s grace and beauty have been captured.

Those who have seen the *Eagle* at sea will find here a reminder not only of her beauty, but of the skill that is required to sail her. For those who will see this ship first in these pages, a fascinating experience in sea lore will unfold in word and picture.

This book was commissioned by the Coast Guard Academy Foundation, a private supporting group of Academy alumni and friends. It is the result of months and years of painstaking research and hard work.

Thousands of color and black-and-white photographs were carefully reviewed before a few dozen were selected. Drawings and blueprints and old sail plans were found hidden deep in archives and stored in nautical museums. For the text, more than twenty years of sailing the *Eagle* were refined into a statement of how a square-rigger functions.

And the voyages retold here are those which actually happened, their accounts reflecting both the *Eagle*'s log and the memories of men who were there.

This is a book of fine seafaring written by a man of sail breeding. It calls to every landlocked Viking and every frustrated Magellan: Come feel the surge of ocean swells, come join the search for freedom and refreshment on blue waters, come seek a renewal of life by returning to the sea.

EMIL "BUS" MOSBACHER, JR.
Skipper of *America's* Cup
Defenders *Weatherly* (1962)
and *Intrepid* (1967)

ACKNOWLEDGMENTS

I have become indebted to so very many people in the process of assembling materials for this book that it is difficult to know where to start, or to stop, in expressing my appreciation.

Certainly, my gratitude must first go to the directors and staff of the Coast Guard Academy Foundation, Incorporated, who commissioned this work. The Foundation is a private, non-profit organization of alumni and friends of the Academy whose express purpose is to provide facilities and services for the Academy and its Cadet Corps, which are not made available from Federal Funds. Through gifts of money, securities and real property, and through such projects as this book, the Foundation seeks to assist the Academy in developing the full potential of each future Coast Guard Officer.

Then, those photographers, both in the Coast Guard and out—amateur and professional—who have contributed to this book cannot be thanked enough. Their interest and their works have created a rich and handsome pictorial story.

As for the text, my first thoughts go to Captain Gordon P. McGowan, USCG retired, and to Van Nostrand Reinhold Company, publishers, for his account of the *Eagle*'s post-war restoration in *The Skipper and the Eagle*. Likewise, I wish to thank Howard I. Chapelle, senior historian at the Smithsonian Institution, and W. W. Norton & Company for a remarkable history of the early Revenue Marine in *The History of American Sailing Ships*. And, of course, my special gratitude to the world's most gifted sea writer, Captain Alan Villiers, for his colorful remarks in *Eagle Sailing*, published by Charles Scribner's Sons.

The editors of *Life* magazine and C. B. Jackson, managing editor of *Oceans* magazine often provided me with insights that had not otherwise occurred to me.

In the search among thousands of photographs for just the right ones, I am particularly grateful to Herbert Wilburn, Jr., illustrations editor, and Thomas R. Smith and Walter Edwards of the National Geographic Society staff. Also Peter J. Braal, manager of photographic illustrations, and Walter Chappelle, education specialist, at Eastman Kodak Company provided great assistance. And from their spectacular television documentary, *Down to the Sea in Ships,* Donald B. Hyatt, director of special projects, and Daniel Jones, Project 21, National Broadcasting Company, offered photographs of unmatched drama.

For the many official Coast Guard photographs, I hope that Elizabeth Segedi, visual information specialist, U.S. Coast Guard Headquarters, and Lieutenant John Shkor, USCG, public information officer at the Coast Guard Academy, will share my appreciation.

The drawings and ship designs of early cutters come from the pen of Henry Rusk and from the endless research, again, of Howard Chapelle. To each, I am much obliged.

And in other matters of history, my good friends Paul Johnson, librarian, and Robert Dixon, Jr., his assistant, at the Coast Guard Academy, provided welcome service. Here, too, I must thank Veryl P. Bevelacqua, who shares my love of maritime traditions, for his thorough knowledge of the naval history that was made along New England's coast.

A constant inspiration and guiding light was Captain Robert L. Davis, USCG, special assistant to the superintendent of the Academy, without whom this project would not have been undertaken, and most certainly not concluded.

In addition to these individuals, there are numerous others who assisted without hesitation on many occasions through their institutions. Thus, I am profoundly obligated to the staffs and members of the New York Yacht Club; Essex Institute, Salem, Massachusetts; Mystic Seaport Museum, Mystic, Connecticut; Massachusetts Historical Society, Boston; Library of Congress, Washington; United States Naval Institute, Annapolis, Maryland; Peabody Marine Museum, Salem, Massachusetts, and the South Street Seaport Museum, New York City.

Finally, I wish to express my gratitude to George E. Ross for his criticism, encouragement and suggestions, and to Mrs. Dona Welch, a diligent and thorough secretary.

WILLIAM IVERSON NORTON

Mystic, Connecticut
February 19, 1970

INTRODUCTION

In flight, an eagle is a creature of singular grace and feathered majesty, soaring from its cliffside eyrie to dizzying heights above the crested sea. Drifting on its broad and sweeping wingspan, guided by the shifting winds, this nearly extinct attendant of Zeus becomes a wondrous spectacle of freedom and strength.

The eagle is, as well, a symbol of the power and courage and independence of the American nation. Since 1782, when its form was emblazoned on the coat of arms of the post-Revolution Congress of Confederation, the eagle has remained a heraldic emblem of the very character and traditions of the American people.

Today, another eagle—it too among the last of its kind—passes from the shelter of hills and shore to brace before the changing winds and venture upon the beckoning sea.

This *Eagle,* the square-rigged training ship of the United States Coast Guard Academy, is a lone and handsome reminder of the long line of ships and seafaring men that made America one of the great maritime nations of the world. With 20,000 feet of sun-bleached canvas taut against a fresh breeze, her golden figurehead in flight above the endless dash of briny swells, this *Eagle* is a ship worthy of continuing the heritage spawned by Nantucket whalers hunting the oceans and sleek Salem clippers racing around Cape Horn for the Orient's riches. But this *Eagle* is more than a symbol of one nation's achievements on the oceans, she is the embodiment of every mariner's belief that the arts of seamanship and the lore and love of sea life are best learned on the decks and in the rigging of sailing ships.

In years past, when hundreds of sailing ships harbored and piloted along America's coasts and navigated every sea and ocean of the world, indoctrination under sail did not have to be arranged. Apprentice seamen, midshipmen and officer-aspirants learned their skills working aboard sail vessels. But the coming of steam and diesel power soon retired those great sailing ships and left few places where young men could learn seamanship in the classic manner—before the mast.

For those who would go down to the sea, training in sailing ships has always served two purposes. First, the ships' officers believe such experience gives apprentices the best possible introduction to all the hazards and pleasures of seafaring. Secondly, the open decks and exposed rigging of a sailing ves-

Eagle's *original golden figurehead.*

sel are at all times public. What is done there, by everyone, is in full view of every officer and every crewman aboard the ship.

Thus, the United States Coast Guard, which has always required exceptional qualities of character and expertise in its officers, was one of the first maritime services in any country to employ sailing ships for the schooling of officer-cadets. The original Coast Guard training ship was the *James C. Dobbin,* a quick and lovely top-sail schooner commissioned for her training mission in 1877. That ship tested initiative, developed enterprise and demanded teamwork of her crew. Under Captain J. A. Henriques, his two lieutenants and a few "intelligent petty officers," the officer-cadets aboard her were provided with an opportunity to prove their mettle.

Those young men and the *Dobbin* did so well that she was soon replaced by a sailing vessel designed especially for the purpose, the 250-ton clipper-like bark *Salmon P. Chase.* For thirty years after her launching in 1878, the *Chase* was a regular feature of Coast Guard life from Buzzards Bay off Massachusetts to Maryland's Chesapeake Bay.

During the first several winters of her operation, cadets went ashore and continued their training in an old sail loft near New Bedford, Massachusetts. Later, the students continued studying in the classrooms on board while the ship lay at anchor in southern ports during the harsh New England winters. Part of each of those years was spent in long cruises under sail, frequently to Europe.

When her time was up, the *Chase* was followed by the auxiliary cutter *Itasca* in 1907, and then by the *Alexander Hamilton.* This barkentine-rigged former naval gunboat named *Vicksburg* had been launched in 1898. The *Hamilton* made a worthy school ship and carried on the Coast Guard's sail training until 1930.

Though the *Hamilton* was not replaced with another training vessel, the Coast Guard's tradition of apprenticeship under sail continued in a fleet of dinghies, sloops and seagoing schooners. Included were a two-masted Gloucester fishing schooner renamed *Chase* and a 65-foot schooner yacht, *Curlew.* Sailing from the Coast Guard Academy in New London, Connecticut, those vessels were put to good use in cruises and races to Block Island, Nantucket, New York and Annapolis.

During World War II, the famous three-masted ocean racing schooner *Atlantic* and the Danish full-rigged ship *Danmark* provided under-sail training. The *Danmark* had been at sea on her annual long cruise when her homeland was invaded by the Germans. Anchored in American waters, her captain, Knud L. Hansen, elected to remain, and the ship was sailed to New London, where she performed excellent service for several years. For a time, Captain Alan Villiers' full-rigged *Joseph Conrad* was also in the Academy's sail-training fleet.

For more than a score of years now, each time the *Eagle* has set her sails and put New London astern, other young men have come to know the sea from her decks and her tops. Each time she has re-emphasized the Coast Guard's belief in sail training and renewed a practice of other Coast Guard school ships. Each time she has reflected, too, the adventurous legacy left by previous American sailing ships whose name she proudly bears.

In the pages that follow, the officers and cadets of the *Eagle* offer an opportunity few people in this age of atoms and space exploration can ever hope to have—a chance to share this heritage and live life at sea aboard one of the last great square-rigged sailing ships.

By word and drawing and picture, the *Eagle* and her crew recall the challenge of rounding a Long Island point more than 100 years ago in a small Yankee cutter to engage an 18-gun British brig. They beckon the most confirmed landlubber and the briniest of skippers to brave a hurricane-swept Atlantic, to lay aloft and man the yards, to learn every sailing maneuver and mariner's skill. These men and their ship invite those who embrace a love of the sea to venture with them in ports-of-call from Bermuda to Copenhagen, to stand with them on a starlit midnight watch, to ride out a whipping gale or snooze in a trade-winds sun. These things, and many more, are the experiences which make up *Eagle Ventures*.

Welcome Aboard!

Building the first Revenue Cutter Massachusetts *at Newburyport, from a mural in the Coast Guard Academy Library, painted by Aldis B. Browne, 1935-1937.*

BUILDING *First Rev Cutter* Massachusetts AT NEWBURYPORT

The heavy morning fog rolled up from the Merrimac River shrouding Plum Island Point in its chilling mist and dampening the clay and cobblestone streets of Newburyport's waterfront. In the waterside yards of William Searle, several shipwrights and a sturdy blacksmith moved among the piles of oak timbers and wrought-iron hardware to begin another day's work on a nearly completed schooner for the new Revenue Marine.

Only a year before, Alexander Hamilton, the first Secretary of the Treasury, had asked the United States Congress to create a fleet of quick sailing ships to help the young nation collect customs duties and enforce its revenue laws. The same hearty Yankees who had cheerfully dumped chests of English tea into Boston Harbor because they objected to paying the duties charged on it by a distant government were equally disgruntled, sometimes, to pay the duties enacted by their own government. But they wanted the tea and other goods, and smuggling had become widespread. Before and during the Revolution, in fact, smuggling had been a patriotic act, even employing a few of the signers of the Declaration of Independence. Yet the new country required the import duties and tonnage dues from the ships and their cargoes, and the smuggling had to be stopped.

To assist Hamilton and the local revenue collectors, the Congress had authorized, in 1790, the construction of ten cutters to operate as the Revenue Marine, the service which decades later became the United States Coast Guard. Each of these cutters was built within the limits of her proposed station. The choice of design and builder, in fact, the whole contract, was largely in the hands of the local collector until the captain was appointed.

The ship being built at Newburyport was one of the ten original vessels and was destined for service off the Massachusetts coast. Although her captain had the builders alter the vessel during construction, she was completed in several months as a two-masted schooner with deep bulwarks and a long quarterdeck. Commissioned the *Massachusetts,* she measured 50 feet on deck with an 18-foot beam and eight-foot depth of hold. Her figurehead was a bust of an Indian, and she had a square stern and carved quarterbadges.

The *Massachusetts* was soon joined by the *Vigilant* in New York, the *General Greene* in Philadelphia, *Scammel* in Portsmouth and *Active, Virginia, South Carolina, Diligence, Pickering* and *Ferret.* Although all were called "cutters" after the English rig and type of vessel publicly associated with

United States Revenue Cutter Active, *among the first ten built.*

revenue collection, nine of these ships were constructed, with the American national rig, as schooners. One, the *General Greene,* was rigged as a sloop.

As soon as these cutters were under construction orders were issued for their service. These specified that the cutters were to cruise—not to anchor in port—and were to patrol their stations in such a way that their movements could not be calculated by smugglers. In 1792, the revenue collectors in ports to which cutters had been assigned were permitted to direct the movements of the vessels within their stations.

During their first eight years of service, these ten cutters were not only the Revenue Marine, they were the American Navy as well. When some 60 to 80 French privateers based at Guadeloupe in the West Indies continued to molest American ships, the young nation blustered into an undeclared war against her former ally, France. With these and several new cutters heavily out-gunned, the United States Navy was formed to meet the French threats and encroachments. Hastily acquiring 54 ships-of-the-line, the new Navy employed eight Revenue cutters. These escorted the famed *Constitution* on her maiden voyage and, throughout the conflict, convoyed American merchantmen. That assignment to cooperate with the Navy established a custom which has been followed in all subsequent wars and continues today.

The naval war with France was a strange series of battles that depended on sailing skill and bluff as much as on gunfire. About 50 American vessels were divided into four squadrons, but strategy dictated that each ship sail an independent course. With a fleet of several French ships sometimes chasing an equal number of American merchantmen escorted by naval ships, American vessels were often bespeaking each other, and prizes on both sides were often retaken. Though some ships never met the enemy, the fast and easily maneuverable Revenue cutters captured more than their share.

One of those valiant little cutters was a fore-and-main topsail schooner named *Eagle*. Designed by Josiah Fox and built at Philadelphia in 1798 by William and Abra Brown, this 187-ton vessel was 58 feet along her keel, 20 feet across her beam, with a nine-foot hold. Her crew included 14 marines. Fourteen six-pounder cannons sprouted through her gun ports.

Captain of this first *Eagle* was Hugh Campbell of South Carolina, a demanding but efficient master of his ship. He did not fear to challenge Secretary of the Navy Benjamin Stoddert who, before the captain deemed her ready for sea, ordered

the ship to join the 20-gun *Montezuma* under Captain Alexander Murray and two other vessels at Norfolk, Virginia. These ships were to cruise in the West Indies protecting American merchant vessels.

Montezuma sailed without *Eagle*, and Secretary Stoddert, rather piqued at Captain Campbell's delay, ordered him to cruise the coasts of Georgia and South Carolina.

Campbell's later record in the West Indies raised the Secretary's low opinion of the master to such heights that in July, 1799, Captain Campbell was commissioned a Navy master commandant. In October, 1800, he was made a Navy captain, which at that time was two grades higher than a captain in the Revenue Marine.

The following November, Campbell was selected to command the 28-gun Navy frigate *General Greene,* replacing Captain Christopher R. Perry, the father of the famous commodores. Captain Campbell was relieved on the Revenue cutter *Eagle* by Lieutenant Simmones Bunbury from Maryland. During the later Barbary Wars, Campbell was raised to the command of the famous Navy frigates *Constellation* and *Constitution,* and from 1805 until 1807 was Commodore of the Mediterranean Squadron.

In the West Indies from 1798 to 1800, this first *Eagle* was one of the most successful ships, first in the squadron of Stephen Decatur, Sr., later in that of Commodore John Barry. In all, the *Eagle* captured five well-armed French vessels. One of her best captures was the schooner *Bon Père* which was renamed *Bee* and used by the American forces. On two other occasions she helped the ships *Delaware* and *Baltimore* take prizes. The cutter also recaptured seven American merchantmen taken by the French privateers, and assisted in taking another ten French vessels.

No further actions involving the *Eagle* were recorded after Lieutenant Bunbury took command of her at the end of December, 1800. The struggle on the seas with France was drawing to a close, and the new skipper was told to "treat public and private armed vessels of France exactly as you find they treat American trading vessels."

The undeclared war had cost the infant government more than six million dollars, and as part of the post-war reduction in arms, the first *Eagle* was sold at Baltimore in June, 1801, for $10,600.

While the combat at sea continued with France for several years, friction with England in matters of trade and ocean commerce had steadily increased since the American Revolution. In the beginning, only a polite diplomatic campaign had been waged by the new republic aimed at wresting from Britain a fair share of the trade with continental Europe. By the turn of the century, however, grievances increased. American seamen, when ashore in British ports, were impressed into service on British ships. England, then at war with France, demanded and exercised her right to search the neutral American ships and often seized anything considered to be contraband.

This subjugation by the Crown just 30 years after the Revolution inflamed the independent spirit of the Yankee seamen, and on June 18, 1812, President James Madison declared that a state of war existed.

During the first two years of the War of 1812, Britain was too busy fighting France to spare many warships, but when Napoleon was exiled to Elba in the spring of 1814, and the Battle of Waterloo was only a year away, the American coast was blockaded by the full power of the Royal Navy. Revenue cutters, again cooperating with the United States Navy, did their best to protect the eastern seaboard and permit some coastal commerce.

By the autumn of 1814, several British ships had been captured, and two Revenue cutters had been lost to the enemy.

A second cutter to carry the name *Eagle* met the enemy bravely, but she, too, became a victim of superior British forces. That *Eagle* was a relatively new schooner of 130 tons purchased for the Port of New Haven in 1809. She was armed with four four-pounders and a pair of two-pounders, and was commanded by Captain Frederick Lee. During the War of 1812, her assignment was to convoy American merchant ships through Long Island Sound. British men-of-war under the daring command of the same Captain Thomas Hardy in whose arms Admiral Lord Nelson had died at the Battle of Trafalgar, often entered the Sound in pursuit of American vessels.

One of the several packets that plied the Sound between New York and New Haven was the sloop *Susan*, home-ported in New Haven and under the command of a Captain Miles. She was returning to New Haven in the dawn of a gray October morning, 1814, hoping to make the best use of the low offshore fog as a seaward camouflage. Her cargo included valuable stores of flour, gunpowder and dry goods, and she carried 16 passengers bound for New Haven. From the fog bank a dashing sloop-tender from the British frigate *Pomone*

DEFENDING THE Eagle IN THE WAR OF 18...   SUPPRESSING Gulf PIRATES

caught the morning breezes and soon overtook the *Susan,* capturing her without so much as firing a shot.

Eagle's Captain Lee, upon hearing of the incident, quickly recruited about 30 volunteers from the waterfront homes and shops of New Haven to reinforce the *Eagle*'s crew and gave chase to retake the *Susan.* As the fog lifted, the English 18-gun brig-of-war *Dispatch* appeared accompanied by her armed tender and a sloop and, in turn, chased the *Eagle.* The dwindling morning breezes prevented the cutter from out-maneuvering the far-superior assembly of British guns, so Captain Lee wisely headed for the Long Island shore and beached the schooner beneath a bluff at Negroes Head.

The crew and volunteers dragged two of the four-pounder guns and both of the *Eagle*'s two-pounders up onto the bluff in an effort to defend their ship. Through broadside and cannonade, cannonade and broadside, the battle flamed for hours. When the British were unable to drive the men off the hillside, they turned their guns upon the cutter in an attempt to destroy it.

But the adamant Yankees were not to be undone, and they remained to stand off repeated attacks, which continued all day and into the night. At one point, wadding for their guns was completely used up. Under the flare of exploding shells, they tore up bits of cloth from their own clothing and even ripped pages from the *Eagle's* log to provide the needed packing. Frequently, they picked up the enemy's shot from the ground and fired it back. Through it all, the American flag was kept flying, though at least twice it took great heroic acts to keep it so.

By the next morning the *Dispatch* and her attendants had been forced to withdraw and what was left of the smolder-ing cutter was refloated by the New Haven men. Still, the worn crew could not keep her from the superior forces against them. Before she could make New Haven, the second *Eagle* was finally taken.

The ravages of war with Britain seriously reduced the number of Revenue cutters, so that when peace finally came, new construction was necessary. The Treasury Department asked William Doughty, a naval architect and constructor, to design three new classes of cutters in 1815. As was usual with his designs, these cutters were on the Baltimore clipper model. Plans called for vessels of three sizes, the smallest was of 31 tons burthen with a 49-foot deck, 15-foot beam and a five-foot depth of hold. The next largest design was 51 tons by Custom House measurement and was 57 feet in length on

Left: Defending the second Eagle *during the War of 1812. Right: The Revenue Marine suppressing pirates on the Gulf of Mexico. Both from a mural in the Coast Guard Academy Library painted by Aldis B. Browne.*

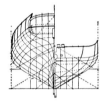

A United States Revenue Cutter
of 31 45/95 Tons and one Gun 1815

Redrawn from a copy, dated May 12, 1815, of a
draught by Wm Doughty
Ref USN-C&R Nº 109-4-10 D

Principal Dimensions :		Spars					
			Whole Length	Dia	Head		Whole Length
Length between perpendiculars	46'3"	Mainmast	48'6"	12"	4'0"	Topmast	14'0"
Length on the range of deck	48'6"	Foremast	47'0"	12¼"	4'0"	Topmast	14'0"
Beam moulded	14'6"	Mainboom	29'0"			Gaffs	10'0"
Depth in the hold	5'0"	Bowsprit	9'0" outboard			Jibboom	9'0" from cap
Custom House Tonnage	Nº 31 45/95 Tons	Squaresail Yard	29'0"			Flying Topsl Yard	15'0"

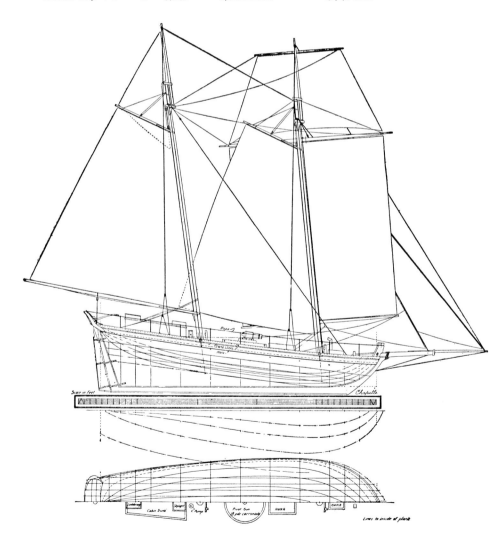

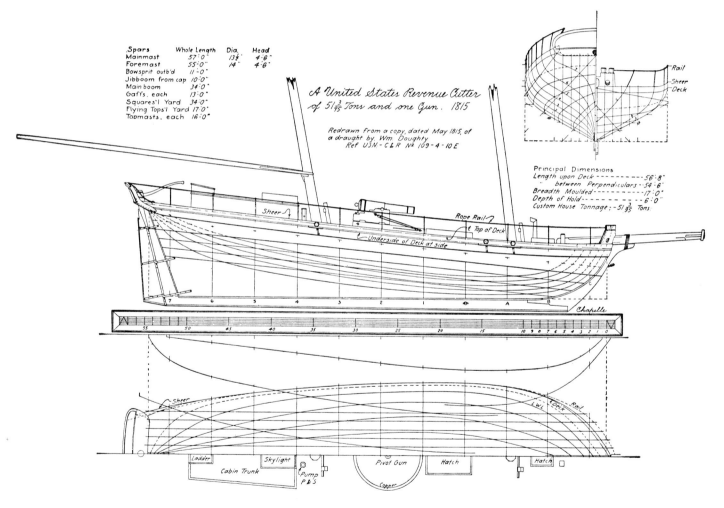

Spars   Whole Length   Dia.   Head
Mainmast   57'·0"   13½"   4'·6"
Foremast   55'·0"   14"   4'·6"
Bowsprit outb'd   11'·0"
Jibboom from cap   10'·0"
Main boom   34'·0"
Gaffs, each   13'·0"
Squares'l Yard   34'·0"
Flying Tops'l Yard   17'·0"
Topmasts, each   16'·0"

A United States Revenue Cutter
of 51 3/95 Tons and one Gun. 1815

Redrawn from a copy, dated May 1815, of
a draught by Wm. Doughty
Ref USN-C&R Nº 109-4-10E

Principal Dimensions
Length upon Deck --------- 56'·8"
    "   between Perpendiculars - 54'·6"
Breadth Moulded ----------- 17'·0"
Depth of Hold ------------- 6'·0"
Custom House Tonnage; - 51 3/95 Tons.

Sheer

Rope Rail

℄ Top of Deck

Underside of Deck at side

Rail
Sheer
Deck

Chapelle

Sheer   LWL   LOCK   Rail

Ladder   Skylight   Pivot Gun   Hatch   Hatch
Cabin Trunk   Pump P&S   Copper

*Opposite: William Doughty's
plans for a 31-ton Revenue
Cutter.
Above: Doughty's drawings
for a 51-ton Revenue Cutter,
circa 1815.*

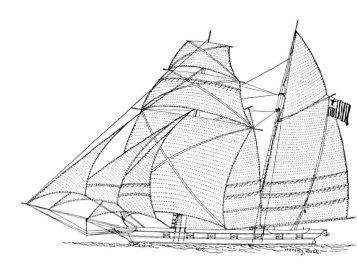

deck with an extreme beam of 17 feet and a depth of hold equaling six feet. A cutter of 79 tons and 69 feet of deck length was the largest design. This vessel had a beam of 19 feet and a seven-foot hold. All the designs were similar, differing but slightly in hull form. Their armament varied, some having 12- or 18-pounder carronades, or long 9-, 12- or 18-pounders. All the cutters' guns were made of brass. A pivot-gun amidships, if not always the sole gun, was always the heaviest.

The third and fourth Revenue cutters named *Eagle* were constructed from Doughty's largest plan. Although little is known about the operations of these two cutters, records show that one was built at New York in 1816 and was intended for service in Boston but was assigned instead to New Haven until 1824. The other, built in 1824, probably at Portsmouth, New Hampshire, was also stationed at New Haven, where she saw duty until 1829. Both of these cutters were commended by the same Frederick Lee who had been skipper of the ill-fated second *Eagle* during the War of 1812.

These two Revenue cutters were used for the routine duties of collecting customs fees, capturing contraband and slave-runners and rescuing life and property endangered by storms or mishaps at sea.

Nearly a century passed before another American ship carried the proud name *Eagle*. The Revenue Marine had become the United States Coast Guard and the age of sailing ships had reluctantly given way to steam and diesel power on the oceans.

The fifth *Eagle,* a vessel for which the name had been revived, was a 100-foot motor patrol boat built at Bay City, Michigan, by Defoe Boat and Motor Works. One of thirteen of her class, she was commissioned on November 11, 1925. A month later this *Eagle* arrived at her assignment, New London, Connecticut, and there, for the following seven years, was engaged in enforcing an unpopular American law—Prohibition.

This ship had a 210-ton displacement, a 23-foot beam and an eight-foot draft. She was equipped with two diesel engines which drove her at ten knots, a speed unfortunately not fast enough to catch many of the rum-runners. Her armament was a single three-inch gun of 23 calibers, which was sufficient to stop anything in her range.

New London was the home of the Coast Guard's Base Four, one of the busiest of the service's rum-chasing facilities. An estimated one-third of all liquor smuggled into the country

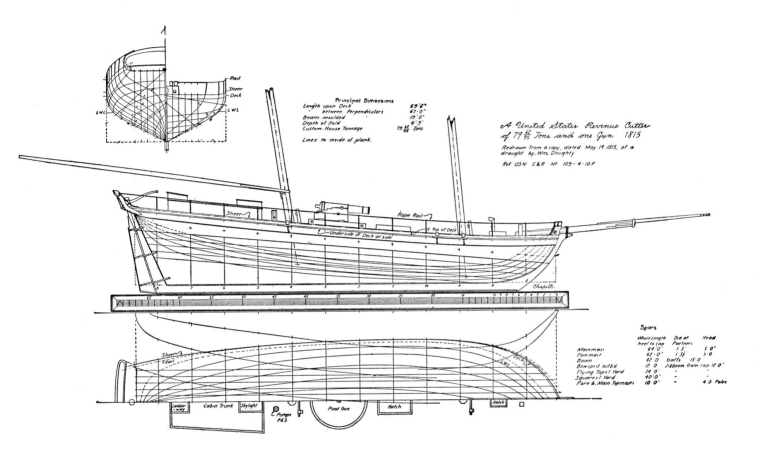

Principal Dimensions

Length upon Deck	69'6"
between Perpendiculars	67'0"
Beam moulded	19'0"
Depth of Hold	8'9"
Custom House Tonnage	79 $\frac{62}{95}$ Tons

Lines to inside of plank.

A United States Revenue Cutter of 79 $\frac{62}{95}$ Tons and one Gun 1815

Redrawn from a copy, dated May 19 1815, of a draught by Wm Doughty

Ref USN C&R Nº 109-4-10F

Spars

	Whole Length heel to cap	Dia at Partners	Head
Mainmast	64'0"	13"	5.0"
Foremast	62'0"	13¼"	5.0"
Boom	42.0	Gaffs	15.0
Bowsprit outb'd	12.0	Jibboom from cap 12.0"	
Flying Tops'l Yard	24.0		
Squares'l Yard	40'0"		
Fore & Main Topmasts	10.0"		4.0 Poles

Opposite: United States Revenue Cutter Forward, *from a sailmaker's advertisement in the collection of M.V. Brewington, Jr.*

Above: Doughty's plans for an 80-ton Revenue Cutter from which the third and fourth Eagles *were constructed.*

in the 1920s came from the notorious Rum Row, an anchorage of supply ships just beyond the three-mile limit. The fast and smaller contact boats swarmed to those ships from New England harbors and inlets. They kept an increasing fleet of Coast Guard craft engaged picketing contact boats and an occasional brazen supply ship until the contraband alcohol could be seized. Such picketing, seizure and search comprised the duties assigned to the fifth American *Eagle*.

A typical incident in this *Eagle*'s rum-chasing career occurred one dark, rainy night in the late 1920s about 40 miles southwest of Nantucket. *Firelight,* a rum ship, or "black," as such ships were popularly called, was already known to the Coast Guard. She had been taken a year earlier and her crew convicted of smuggling, but released by a typically lenient court. Just before midnight, the *Eagle* took over trailing the "black" from a destroyer also stationed at Base Four. As was often the case, the larger ship could not pursue the "rummie" among the islands and shoals off the Rhode Island coast.

The cutter started picketing at midnight. About twenty minutes later, *Firelight* swerved, opened her engines full and came at the *Eagle,* which was drifting nearby. The cutter quickly reversed her engines to avoid the charging "black," but her starboard side was still struck lightly.

No serious damage was done to the cutter, but the rum-runners had misjudged the comparative strength of the two craft. Their own ship began to sink, her underwater planking broken and parted. The eight men aboard *Firelight* jumped into the ebony water, where they were later picked up and taken to New London to face charges.

In September, 1932, the fifth *Eagle* was given a permanent change of duty station to Charleston, South Carolina, where she continued in activities similar to those she had been performing in New London. However, a new presidential administration elected that year doomed the "noble experiment" of Prohibition, and other duties were found for the cutter the following July at Charlotte, New York, on the shores of Lake Ontario. After a year at that station, the ten-year-old ship was sold.

Before another American ship would carry the proud "Eagle" name to sea, the nation would suffer a debasing economic depression, and two-thirds of the world would be laid asunder by a global war of unmatched ferocity. More than fifteen years would pass before "Eagle" was again emblazoned on a Coast Guard cutter.

ON OR ABOUT 18 JANUARY 1946 PROCEED BY AIR TO LONDON ENGLAND AND REPORT TO COMNAVEU FOR FURTHER ASSIGNMENT AS PROSPECTIVE COMMANDING OFFICER OF THE COAST GUARD CUTTER EAGLE NOW THE GERMAN EX-NAVAL SHIP HORST WESSEL AT THE U S NAVAL ADVANCE BASE WESER RIVER BREMERHAVEN GERMANY.

With this telegraphed message, Commander Gordon P. McGowan, United States Coast Guard, received orders to head a group of ten officers and Coast Guardsmen as the nucleus of a crew to restore and bring to the United States a war-torn square-rigged sailing ship which would sail again under the American flag and bear the cherished name, "Eagle."

Some weeks before, the Superintendent of the Coast Guard Academy had heard that the German fleet, though largely destroyed during World War II, was to be divided up as war reparations. He knew that among the prizes-of-war there was a three-masted bark—a ship capable of continuing the Coast Guard's tradition of training under sail.

So Commander McGowan, two junior line officers, one engineering officer and several petty officers were dispatched to Germany to repair the ship and make her ready to sail back to the Academy at New London.

Little were they aware of how difficult it would be in the next five months to outfit a sailing ship amid the destruction of post-war Germany, or how hazardous a voyage home they would face when caught in a hurricane off Bermuda.

Arriving in Bremerhaven, Commander McGowan found the ship he was to command lying at a bombed-out shipyard surrounded by ugly skeletons of shattered buildings and mountainous heaps of rubble. Her stately masts were canted drunkenly to starboard as she rested on the bottom of a narrow channel at low tide. Her gray sides were smeared with stains and the paint on her yards and masts was blistered and cracked. Raised lettering on each side of the quarterdeck proclaimed to the world that this was the *Horst Wessel,* a dying ship of the dead German Navy.

The *Horst Wessel,* which was named after a young Nazi leader, had been built at the Blohm and Voss shipyard in Hamburg and launched in 1936 with *der Führer* in attendance. She was a three-masted bark, 295 feet in length and displaced 1,800 tons. She had an auxiliary diesel which could be disengaged from the propeller while under sail.

The German Navy operated four such vessels in the 1930s, all bark-rigged. One was lost at sea during the war, and the *Horst Wessel*'s sister ship, the *Albert Leo Schlageter* remained

*Hitler attended the gala
christening of the* Horst
Wessel *in 1936. Photo from*
Die Yacht, *Vol. 31, No. 10,
published in Berlin, 1936.*

at Bremerhaven unclaimed during the fitting out of her twin. Eventually, she was restored and transferred to Brazil. A third bark, the *Gorch Foch,* went to the Soviet Union.

For three years the *Horst Wessel* had served the Germans as a training ship, making cruises to the Canary Islands and the West Indies. When Germany made its belligerent moves in 1939, the ship remained in the vicinity of the Baltic Sea. At the outbreak of World War II she was confined entirely to the Baltic, sometimes transporting supplies to and refugees from East Prussia. Her log records that at least once she fired at Allied aircraft, and that Adolf Hitler's birthday was dutifully observed on board.

At the very end of the war, the ship narrowly escaped total destruction by failing to arrive at her port of destination on time. She had been directed to proceed to Kiel, and arriving near the harbor entrance after dark, lay off shore until daylight. That fateful night an enormous air raid hit the area. A rain of incendiary bombs did frightful damage ashore, and sank every vessel in the harbor. Seeing the impossibility of carrying out his orders, the captain proceeded independently to Flensburg, where the vessel remained the few days that were left of the war.

The remnants of the German Navy, including the *Horst Wessel,* had been turned over to the Allied Forces in a simple and well-ordered manner. Assurances had been given that the Germans would not engage in sabotage, and therefore, the crews were allowed to remain with their ships. Many assisted in disarming the vessels and disposing of ammunition and other explosives.

When Commander McGowan and his party arrived at Bremerhaven, the *Horst Wessel* was still manned by her German crew. Using that crew and the nearby Rickmers' Werft shipyard force as manpower, the Americans proceeded with the fitting out.

Repairing the *Horst Wessel* was officially a project of the United States Navy, under whose control she was to remain until sailing day. At that time, she was transferred to the Coast Guard's jurisdiction. Thus, during the restoration period, Commander McGowan had no official authority to give orders—he could only object to work he thought unsatisfactory and refuse to take the ship to sea. From the beginning, however, he discovered that he would have a free hand in repairing the ship, and to the end, there was never a controversy with the Navy.

The two big problems confronting the Americans were:

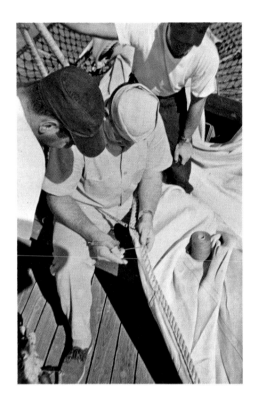

where could they get material things such as tools, spare parts, sail cloth, ropes and lines of various sizes and—the intangible ingredient—the know-how necessary to take a square-rigger across the Atlantic unescorted. The officers and crew set to work dividing their time between searching out the tangibles and studying the operation of the complex rigging aloft.

Commander McGowan's first action was to thoroughly inspect the ship accompanied by the former skipper, a dignified 35-year-old German with the rank of *kapitain-leutnant*. Days and weeks of constant association between the two officers were gradually to change their relationship from one of cool politeness to something bordering on friendship and admiration for each other and the ship.

The inspection revealed that work to be done on the vessel would fall into three parts. First, and most important, was obtaining sails and seeing to it that the rigging was in proper condition. Second was the installation of a new engine block, reassembling the main engine and generally putting things in order down below. Third was scrounging for all the spare parts and gear the crew could lay its hands on. The bosun's locker, for example, contained pitiful leftovers testifying to the shortness of replacement lines and deck stores toward the end of the war. When it was inspected, the welcome aroma of oakum and pine tar filled the air, but the lockers and bins were empty. A few old coils of line, a couple of dull, badly worn marlinspikes, fragments of beeswax and a rawhide mallet worn down to the metal retaining ring were all that could be found. The same signs of poverty were painfully evident in the sail locker. The sails were there, but they were old and worn and bore many patches.

Most of the equipment still on board had no counterpart on the American market, so once the spares that the crew could take along were used up, a worn machine or rigging would have to be replaced with custom-made components.

The fitting out was further complicated by instructions to the prospective captain that the ship should be made seaworthy in all respects at no cost to the American government. This meant that all sail cloth, spare parts and fittings had to come from German establishments. New sails, although readily available in London, Copenhagen or Stockholm, had to be produced in German sail lofts by German sailmakers.

Those restrictions made Commander McGowan and his crew become a cunning, and often greedy, lot.

Word was sent out to all the Allied commands in Germany of the restoration project, and generally, what materials would

Above: The sails were worn and needed much repair.
Right: A new engine block helped put things in order down below.
Right above: Eagle's emergency helm on the fantail.

be needed. In response, tips and rumors abounded, and Commander McGowan and his supply officer were sent off on many a wild goose chase. Frequently their searches led to burned warehouses or bombed-out buildings still shown on paper as containing the sought-after marine hardware.

At first they went to a particular place to look for a particular item, but it was not long before that sort of effort proved to be a waste of time. Their treasure hunt had to be an independently conducted job for a true opportunist. Only after what seemed to be many wasted trips into the country-side by the supply officer, did ship's stores begin to roll in. Sometimes the flow would be reduced to a trickle. Occasionally, he would hit the jackpot.

Some 22 miles of Manila line plus bins full of new marlinspikes, fids and mallets, turnbuckles, bolts and shackles were found in an old warehouse at Columbus Key, a former berthing spot for the German liners *Bremen* and *Europa* and a familiar pre-war tourist mecca.

At Augsburg, where the *Horst Wessel's* original engine had been forged, the British were using the same facilities to supply their minesweepers in the North Sea. When a suitable diesel engine was found, the British were persuaded to make certain alterations, and the problem of a new engine block was solved.

Likewise, a persistent search far inland led to the several thousand meters of fresh sail cloth, and a short time later, enough sail twine to supply the ship for years to come.

In Hamburg, German sailmakers from five old sailmaking guilds were employed to complete the new canvas for the ship. Working in a partially bombed-out sail loft, they endured the foul weather that winter and early spring brings to the northern German coast. Though sometimes nearly blue with cold and often weak from lack of food, they stitched and sewed as best they could until the huge sails took shape. The last canvas was finished only one day before the ship sailed for home.

Six weeks after Commander McGowan and his advance guard landed in Germany, the second American group arrived by ship. In that group, along with the new executive officer and an electrical engineering specialist, were about 50 downy-cheeked apprentice seamen, many of whom had never been to sea before. In the United States, post-war demobilization was in full swing and the manpower needed from America to safely sail the ship home was just not going to come. A few days later, McGowan was notified that the expected

"Lay out, and furl her in."

cadets from the Academy would not be able to help because of more important assignments at home.

With no authority to employ Germans to sail the ship, and with too few Americans to work her safely, it began to look as though the project was doomed to failure. But the new captain was determined, so he continued and hoped for the best.

Taking stock of the situation only made things seem blacker. The skipper was a novice in square-riggers. The executive officer, an excellent seaman, was limited in experience to small-boat sailing. The two junior officers had much the same background. The engineering officer was primarily a steam man, whereas the machinery down below was diesel, and the deck force were all green hands at sea. The two boatswain's mates aboard were excellent—one had sailed in commercial fishermen but never in square-riggers.

On the brighter side, the crew and officers were all in good health, they were beginning to learn the operations of their new ship and they had all grown very fond of this vessel with her beautiful lines and deep ancestry in sea lore.

As the weather improved and flowers and patches of green softened the jagged contours of the ruined Bremerhaven shoreline, the heavy repairs on the ship neared completion. During the winter, when icy gale after gale had blown across the ship, the work had been confined to repairs below deck. With better weather, a schedule of outside work was established, including the renewal of rigging.

Tentative sail stations were assigned, since that would also provide training for the new crew. The German sailors were used in key spots where their familiarity with the rigging could best be observed by the green hands. They went through all the operations as graphically as possible for the benefit of the learners.

"Study the rigging all the time," Commander McGowan had told the new men when they arrived. "Your life may depend upon your knowledge of which line to grab and which to keep your hands off while you are aloft."

As a first step in the outside work, the standing rigging was opened and inspected. A few of the shrouds and stays supporting the masts and yards were replaced with new wire rope that had come in from a largely destroyed shipyard near Bremen. The ratlines which run horizontally from shroud to shroud were also replaced. That process is called by a briny term, "rattling down."

The running rigging, consisting of lines that are hauled and slacked and moved about in various ways to favorably match

sail and wind, was renewed with yards of Manila line found at Columbus Key.

The ship was then ready for drydocking. As she settled on the keel blocks and the water receded, her beautiful body was slowly unveiled. She had the underwater lines of a racing yacht, the delicate curving contours of her hull sweeping aft with grace. The Germans beamed with pride and the Americans' eyes lit up in admiration.

As soon as the water was clear of the hull, gangs of men with high pressure hoses washed away the mud and loose barnacles. That was followed by scraping and wire brushing. A thorough inspection revealed that the hull was in good condition and that no major repairs were necessary except to the rudder. The rudder or rudder post or both had been damaged by a near-miss bomb explosion, but their repair turned out to be a rather simple matter of realignment.

The next step was to change the flaking slate-gray hull to the Coast Guard's traditional white, and complete the finishing touches which would beautify a ship that was daily becoming more seaworthy. Somewhere, McGowan's ever-resourceful supply officer found the paint. He also found a supply of cleaning gear, soap and brass polish, and for a few more weeks the crew and workmen had their work cut out for them.

Another task was the translating of nameplates on all the equipment both above and below decks. With typical thoroughness, the Germans had labeled the workings of every compartment of the vessel, making her operations crystal clear to anyone who could read German. But for the homeward passage, these had to be translated into English and new plates manufactured and installed. Luckily, a former engineer for North German Lloyd Lines was found who could do the arduous task. His work was a great blessing in later days when Americans found the fruits of his labors their only source of information.

A final touch to the nearly restored ship was a purely aesthetic one. The ship's figurehead was a massive gold eagle with wings outspread, its talons clutching a wreath in which a swastika had been mounted. The hated "crooked cross" had been removed, however, at the very end of the war. Commander McGowan thought it pure coincidence that the future *Eagle* should have such a figurehead, but the eagle was just another piece of Nazi symbolism and had appeared everywhere. He felt sure that most people at home wouldn't know this, so he planned to point with pride at the handsome

masterpiece. A few days before the new *Eagle* was commissioned, the figurehead was improved further by the gift of a hand-carved teak Coast Guard shield to be mounted within the wreath.

By early May, Commander McGowan and his crew could see that their task of restoration was soon going to be successful and that the many problems encountered during the long German winter would be over.

Still, two crises of which the crew seemed blissfully unaware nagged the captain constantly. It was grim fact that the manpower shortage had not been, and apparently was not going to be, resolved. The ship had been built to carry 220 German cadets, 125 enlisted men and 14 officers. The designers had deliberately worked toward the end of making maximum use of muscle, rather than machinery. To get the anchor up required two teams of 20 men each, one hoisting while the other rested. Muscles, strong backs and teamwork were the only things furnished for the hoisting of her boats, for her braces, sheets, inhauls, outhauls, and for her halyards. Now it seemed this would have to be done by a total of about 60 people, including the captain!

His second worry was the hurricane season, which sometimes starts in the Atlantic as early as June. Unless the ship could be completed and set sail very soon, there would be an increasing likelihood of tangling with one before the voyage was over.

The manpower problem came to an unexpected solution one Sunday afternoon in the naval officers' club. A British officer who had engaged McGowan in a conversation about the ship heard about the need for more hands in the crew. The Britisher told the worried skipper that he was in charge of the minesweeping operations in the North Sea and that he had been using Germans by the hundreds. He offered to "enlist" the Germans aboard the *Eagle* in his minesweeping and "loan" them to the captain while they were needed for the Atlantic crossing. A few days later, through that piece of extraordinary business, the German crew which had helped so much in the restoration was assigned to help sail its former ship to America.

Commander McGowan was so pleased over this stroke of good fortune that he forgot about the hurricanes. He did, however, often wonder how his British savior pulled off his part of the deal without being court-martialed. Apparently, whoever learned of the arrangement must have seen it as a simple solution to a difficult problem.

Tar and pitch fill seams in the teak weather decks.

With this additional crew assured, the prospective captain began to work for the day of commissioning his ship. After careful calculation of the time needed to load stores, get the galley range in proper shape, and make the sleeping quarters habitable, he estimated that the *Eagle* could be commissioned on May 15.

With mounting excitement and increasing activity, the Americans were transferred from the Navy barracks where they had lived for months to their ship. Somehow, by the time the great day was upon them, every detail seemed to be ready. The ship had a gleaming coat of fresh white paint, some of it not yet dry. Her masts were glistening with new buff spar enamel, and the yards were squared with smart precision. Stores and water had been shifted below until she was on an exact even keel. Her masts seemed taller than ever before, reaching for the clear sky and puffs of light clouds overhead.

From the U. S. Naval Command came the commodore, who was piped aboard with all the ceremony the captain and his crew could muster. Along the starboard side, the American enlisted men stood facing inboard. On the port side was the German crew. Lined up athwartships were the officers in double rank, the Americans in front and the Germans behind.

The commodore read his orders directing Commander McGowan to place the ship in commission, and handed them to the new captain. He read his orders and assumed command. With that, all faced aft at salute, and to the accompaniment of shrilling bosun's pipes, the American ensign was hauled smartly to the gaff. With the "making of colors," the executive officer was ordered to "set the watch." The watch standers took their stations, sideboys fell in at the gangway and the commodore left the ship.

Captain McGowan then gave a short talk to his ship's company. The air was charged with emotion. For the Americans, a tremendous adventure was just being launched. To the Germans, this had been an act of finality. The ship that many of them had looked upon as home no longer existed. The Coast Guard cutter *Eagle* was now a vessel of the United States.

As the formation was dismissed, the new captain glanced at the ranks of Germans. They were standing stiff as ramrods, some with tears coursing down their cheeks.

Sailing day came two weeks later. Commander McGowan had received unique orders for the trip home. Had he obeyed them to the letter, he could have gone by way of the Suez

Canal, India, Thailand, and on through the Panama Canal, taking a year or two to make the trip. When received in Bremerhaven, they read something like this: YOU ARE HEREBY GRANTED THE WIDEST POSSIBLE DISCRETION AS TO TIME OF DEPARTURE ROUTE TO BE TAKEN AND PORTS OF CALL AND TIME OF ARRIVAL IN THE UNITED STATES.

After poring over pilot charts, sailing instructions and all the other nautical publications he could get his hands on, the captain chose a much shorter route, and yet, one that was least likely to get the ship in trouble. In general, that route closely paralleled the first voyage of Columbus.

Passage would first be made down the English Channel, then the captain proposed to depart from the southern tip of England, slanting southwestward for Funchal, on the island of Madeira. From Madeira, the *Eagle* would continue on the same approximate heading, using the northwest trade winds and call next at the Canary Islands. From there, she would head due west to St. Thomas in the Virgin Islands. Next would be visits in Miami and Bermuda; thence to New London.

That was the original plan. It was later changed to omit stops at the Canary Islands, St. Thomas and Miami.

The last 14 days in May in Germany were marked by uniformly good weather. All hands agreed that it was so important to get the ship ready for sailing, to make last minute adjustments and to see that all cargo was securely stored, that they worked seven days a week. As a reward, the captain promised them a maximum of privileges in the clean, tropical ports-of-call.

But he knew that the true reward, shared by all, lay in the satisfaction derived from bringing the *Eagle* to life.

On sailing day the officers and men—American and German—were a cocky lot.

Dawn came bright and clear, but with a dead calm.

"I put on a show of being disappointed at not having any breeze," the captain recalled years later, "but the cold truth is I had more than a little bit of a feeling of relief. We would sail under power. The people on the beach would not get a chance to criticize any clumsiness on our part."

The ship was anchored in fairly shallow water and her handpowered windlass got only a brief workout as the crew weighed anchor. The boys at the capstan bars were just getting warmed up when the signal came—"Anchor's aweigh!"

Assisted by a moderate ebb tide, the *Eagle* squared off down the channel of the Weser River with her diesel exhaust

A cadet delivers the noontime mess to be sampled by the cadet officer-of-the-deck. Finding it good, he ate the lot.

barely audible. Toward the outer harbor, the clear morning gave way to a foggy haze, and the watchers on the beach were soon lost to the eye.

It was 700 miles from Bremen to Falmouth and going the distance was tricky business. From the Weser River, the *Eagle*'s course crossed a bay by the North Sea and followed the English Channel down through the Strait of Dover, around the Thames River estuary past Southampton into Falmouth. The entire area had been loaded with mines during the war and was still extremely hazardous despite the constant clearing work of minesweepers. The Channel itself was cluttered with the sunken skeletons of Allied ships.

Through the reminders of disaster, a narrow waterway twisted and wound its way toward the *Eagle*'s first destination. As a precaution against foul weather, which might blow the ship off her precarious course, a German tugboat chugged ahead as an escort.

The first day at sea was crowded with housekeeping chores. Seamen armed with buckets and hand swabs went to work on the decks, paint and brightwork. Down below, others were trying to bring order out of the chaos of the ship's hasty loading. Lashing down loose gear and finishing other temporarily neglected duties, they made the *Eagle* ready for her passage on the open sea ahead.

To starboard, Helgoland passed silent and mysterious, unseen in the fog. To port, the north German coast and the Netherlands slid by unnoted as the *Eagle*'s navigator marked each buoy on his chart, tracking the ship's progress with penciled notations.

As evening fell, a gentle breeze came up from dead ahead. Although the zephyr swept the fog away and brought out the darkening horizon, it also slowed the ship down. An hour later the breeze freshened, bringing movement ahead to a crawl. The *Eagle* then signaled across to the tug for a tow line.

All the second day the wind continued and the ship's expanse of rigging and yards aloft acted as a brake. The *Eagle* would have progressed nowhere without assistance from the tug. As the ship moved southward, the weather became steadily worse.

On the third day out of Bremerhaven the sky clouded over and a cold, misty rain set in, chilling everyone on deck. The southerly wind squeezing through the Strait of Dover picked up speed and held the ship back even more. It seemed to take hours to pass every light or buoy or point.

Finally, the towing hawser was cast off and the tug released as the *Eagle* rounded a point of land just outside the Falmouth harbor entrance at the end of the fourth day. As the harbor pilot boarded the square-rigged vessel, his manner showed keen interest in this out-of-the-ordinary craft. Shortly, the anchor was dropped in the quiet harbor and a feeling of anticlimax swept over the crew. The passage from Germany had been dull and monotonous. It had also been uncomfortable and cold—a far cry from the May thoughts of clear skies and bright sunshine.

Commander McGowan had intended to remain in Falmouth only long enough to take on fuel and ship's stores. However, a storm of considerable strength swept the outer coast of England and forced the ship to stay in port until it passed. Even in the miserable weather, the *Eagle* drew crowds to the waterfront, and often she was surrounded by small boats. Under such admiring eyes, the still-green crew developed a tendency to swagger in the manner of old salts, sometimes purposely shouting a just-learned seaword louder than necessary.

Four days later the storm abated. It was the first week in June and time for the *Eagle* to depart from Land's End. The storm had blown fiercely by, but had left calm weather in its wake. As the ship cleared the headland of Falmouth harbor the captain began to feel the Atlantic swell. There, at last, was the real beginning of the voyage home.

In planning the trip, Commander McGowan had regarded the Bay of Biscay off the coast of Spain and southern France as the most dangerous part of the course. On pilot charts and sailing instructions it is plainly indicated that the weather there is unpredictable and capricious. The bold coast lines pierce into the Atlantic offering few refuges in case a ship is forced to seek shelter. In the days of sail, many ships were wrecked on the leeward shores. As a result, the *Eagle*'s engine was kept chugging along at standard speed during that passage, and no particular wish was made for a breeze to stir the slackened, rolling sea.

Shortly after breakfast on the second day out of Falmouth an excited messenger rapped on the door of the captain's cabin.

"Cap'n, the OD says we got a breeze coming up."

As Commander McGowan arrived on the quarterdeck, he could see, in the path of the morning sun, ripples furrowing the surface of the water. The wind was coming from the port quarter, exactly what all on board had wanted. He watched

"All hands to sail stations!"

for a moment as it freshened, then hesitated in thought. He looked at his executive officer and nodded.

An earlier pre-dawn check with the navigator had told him that a strong current was carrying the *Eagle* toward Madeira faster than they had originally expected, and soon the ship would be clear of the threatening Biscay weather.

He also knew everyone was ready for some action.

The executive officer, an eager expression on his face, picked up a megaphone and called, "All hands to sail stations!"

The crew scrambled to their places.

"Lay aloft, lay out and unfurl!"

Side by side, the Germans and Americans raced up the ratlines and out onto the yards. With feverish excitement, they bellied over the spars and began to unfasten the gaskets. In this light breeze and as recognition of the occasion, the sails were unfurled man-o'-war style, all falling at the same command.

After the unfurling and when all sails were ready for setting, the men in the rigging secured loose ends of the gaskets and swarmed down on deck, where the fun of bracing and hauling began. With great confidence and perhaps too much courage, all sails were set.

As the sails began to draw, the *Eagle* became a thing of beauty. Heeling over slightly to leeward, her lower mizzensails exactly balanced the foretopmast staysails, and like a perfect lady, she curtsied and danced along on the open sea.

In mid-afternoon the order was passed to begin taking off sail, and by sunset all sails were furled except the lower courses and lower topsails. That was a safety precaution. The captain was not about to let his green crew scramble to sail stations in the darkness until each man was completely familiar with every line to be encountered on the way up and on the way down. By allowing only the strongest and safest sails to remain set during the night, an unexpected squall could do little harm. That limitation remained in force all the way to Madeira.

Settling into the routine of life at sea, the crew on the *Eagle* usually started each morning by piling on sail. As soon as it was good daylight—during the four-to-eight watch—the call would ring out: "All hands to sail stations!"

After noses were counted as an added check against someone having fallen overboard during the night, the topgallant and royal sail handlers would lay aloft and loose their respective sails. The remainder of the crew would see to the jibs, staysails and mizzensails. By breakfast time all sails

Above: Housekeeping chores.
Right: Practice with a sextant
makes a fine navigator.

would be set and drawing nicely. Then the ship's cleaning routine would begin.

The decks would get scrubbed and the general housekeeping chores would be done until it was necessary to tack, take off sail, or get involved in some other maneuver connected with following the ship's course.

Every day the *Eagle* sailed farther and farther offshore and was less likely to get ensnarled in the frequent foul weather north of the Gibraltar latitudes.

Occasional French or Spanish fishermen passed, invariably changing their courses and hauling over to have a better look at the white square-rigger. One night a big passenger steamer, lit up like a Christmas tree, steamed by, heading in the general direction of Gibraltar. It was a bright, clear night with the moon low above the eastern horizon.

"I could tell by the ship's maneuvering," Commander McGowan once recalled, "that the captain got us between him and the moon so the passengers could have a good look at our silhouette.

"Only the lower courses and tops'ls were set. I was sorry we didn't have everything on so we could give them a real show."

On the sixth day out of Falmouth the navigator's calculations told the captain that the *Eagle* would arrive off Funchal after dark on the seventh. The main island of Madeira rose steeply out of the ocean and had very deep water close inshore. Funchal was on the lee side, sheltered from the prevailing winds, and thus offered quiet water for anchorage.

As the ship made her landfall, Madeira was cast against the setting sun at the close of a bright subtropical day. The ship approached downwind, and, for the first time since her departure, carried full sail in the darkness. Reaching the sheltered water behind the island before anchoring at Funchal, the men had their first opportunity to prove their skill at manning sail stations at night.

The streets of Funchal hung from the mountainsides, presenting a spectacular view from seaward. Pastel colors, so frequently seen in subtropical ports, abounded on the buildings which, with their tiled roofs, ranged tier upon tier up the steep slopes from the mirroring water. The harbor was almost empty of ships, and across the lush green landscape, the scattered resort hotels mostly offered only boarded windows. Madeira had slept peacefully through the war and still lay undisturbed.

For the next three days the *Eagle*'s crew enjoyed its first

liberty ashore while the captain and officers made the usual courtesy calls on the American consul and local authorities.

At seaside cafes near the city wharf the sailors mixed with the islanders, sitting under colorful umbrellas or basking in the golden sunshine. Some went into the small shops to buy the famous Madeira linen, canary birds or trinkets while others played on the sandy beaches or wandered through forested hills high above the ocean.

Too soon, however, preparations had to begin for the longest part of the crossing home—the 3,000-mile arc to Bermuda.

With water and fuel tanks filled to the brim and the ship's lockers fattened with food, the *Eagle* weighed anchor and headed for sea. In the wind shadow of the island, she was totally becalmed. So, all sails furled, she putt-putted somewhat shamefully into the distance under "bare poles."

By noon of the second day a dramatic change had taken place and the wind approached the ideal—just strong enough for a lively eight knots wearing diagonally downwind—but not strong enough to build a sea of any size.

The trade-wind sky was a greenish-blue, relieved only by high puffs of cloud. Whitecaps gracefully topped each crested wave and bent in rows abeam the ship. With her tall masts stretching skyward, the *Eagle* swept along in silence like a queen in full regalia moving among her bowing subjects to the coronation.

As one brilliant day followed another, the *Eagle* passed no other ships. The pilot charts showed that few steamship lanes crossed that part of the ocean, and from Madeira to Bermuda not a vessel was sighted.

By running before the wind in good conditions of wind and sea, the crew was spared the necessity of working the ship. All attention was devoted to getting the vessel shined up for the arrival home. During the war all brass and bright work had been painted over and the refitting in Germany had not allowed the luxury of uncovering it. Now, the crew made a game of discovering brass, and shining it, and of laying bare velvety-brown areas of teak and applying the satiny finish that handsome wood deserved.

Each day the *Eagle* became shinier and smarter in appearance. And each day the crew became more tanned by the tropical sun and healthier with good food and work.

The Germans kept pretty much to themselves when off duty, but they seemed to be having a fine time. Sounds of singing poured forth through the ventilators from their

Opposite: Eagle's *view of a port-of-call.*
Above: Her tall masts stretching skyward, the Eagle *swept along on a trade-winds sea.*

quarters below. Their withdrawal had no resemblance to clannishness or coolness toward the Americans. Throughout the watches, friendships between men of the two nationalities budded, but the language barrier made close relationships difficult even in the presence of mutual trust and respect.

In the vicinity of the Canary Islands the trade winds curve to the westward and follow the equator. Since the *Eagle* was making good time—about 200 miles a day—Commander McGowan decided to vary his latitude up and down a bit to find the best breezes. As the *Eagle* slanted southward, the breeze began to slacken around Latitude 22. On reversing the process, the ship began to lose it again in Latitude 24. So the skipper chose the halfway point and continued westward under ideal conditions.

The navigator's sights proved that the current was helping the movement as well as the wind. That course was splitting the distance between the doldrums and the horse latitudes, both of which the captain wanted to avoid.

As with almost every voyage, the good sailing weather had to end sometime. The charts on board showed that the beautiful breeze which the *Eagle* had sailed on for days could be held all the way to St. Thomas in the Virgin Islands. This, in fact, had been the original plan. But by cutting the crossing short, the ship had to leave the trade winds and head northward toward Bermuda.

At a point estimated by the navigator to be three days' sailing time from Hamilton harbor, the change of course was made. A day and a half later the ship entered the horse latitudes and the breeze died abruptly. As the breeze failed, the order was given to start the engine and the *Eagle* chugged mournfully along with everything furled in an empty ocean. Her wake followed a perspective line on the liquid mirror to the vanishing point far astern. The smooth ripples of her bow made a perfect V, extending to either quarter beyond the range of sight.

There the world stood still, and the wind no longer existed. Huge cumulus clouds hung motionless in the distance, their expanding towers and embattlements finally reaching the stratosphere. Somewhere below those far displays there were tepid rain squalls, possibly with some momentary wind. The ship's barometer showed that they were well into that area of fairly constant high pressure near Bermuda.

Next day, at the crack of dawn, just as the navigator—and a few others—had predicted, the ship arrived off St. David's Head at the entrance to the channel leading into Hamilton.

In Bermuda the *Eagle* was greeted by the Superintendent of the Academy, an admiral who arrived aboard the Coast Guard cadet practice cruise ship with a full complement of officers and cadets. In port, too, were the first arrivals from the biennial Newport-to-Bermuda yacht race, many of whom were personal friends of the *Eagle*'s captain and the other Academy officers.

It was a spectacular reception for the new ship, and she was ready for it. The work permitted by the long bright days of the passage from Madeira was reflected everywhere. The decks were spotless, the varnish work fore and aft accented by gleaming brass. Even the tiny fragments of hull rust—a price paid for wearing white at sea—had been carefully erased and returned to snowy perfection.

For four days the admiral and his officers toured the ship and entertained guests and friends on board. On July Fourth a gala reception was given by the American consul general at his residence. That occasion was followed by others on board the *Eagle*. As the admiral beamingly showed visitors about the vessel, it soon became evident not only that he was taking great personal pride in the new acquisition, but that she would almost certainly be his home at sea next summer.

When the last guests had left the ship on her final night in Hamilton, the admiral broke the unexpected news to Commander McGowan that he intended to sail with the *Eagle* the next morning and watch the ship in action for the first few hours of the day. He would then transfer to his flagship and they would go their separate ways.

"The admiral likes us too well!" the *Eagle*'s skipper muttered to himself. "He is going to find out all about us, including our flaws, before this is over."

At the first sign of light the *Eagle* began preparations for her last leg toward home. By mid-morning she was ready to sail, and without ceremony, steamed out the Hamilton channel. The admiral came onto the quarterdeck, and although there was absolutely no breeze, expressed a wish to see the sails set. Accordingly, the crew was sent aloft to start unfurling while the vessel was still navigating the channel.

The flagship followed to a point well clear of Bermuda. The intention had been to photograph the *Eagle* in all her splendor and from every angle with all sails set, but the weather was most unaccommodating. What hint of breeze there had been in the early morning died away, leaving the ship in a dead calm.

Commander McGowan wanted to abandon the effort right

A cadet honor guard welcomes special guests on board.

there, but the admiral's eagerness to see everything set was so keen that he insisted the crew go ahead in hope that some breeze might spring up.

One by one, the men set all the sails—and the ship lay dead in the water slatting about in the swells made by the flagship as it steamed back and forth relentlessly photographing the *Eagle* in all her shame. The sails hung like flour sacks; blocks clattered against the standing rigging.

After a couple of hours of that, the admiral finally gave the welcome word that the *Eagle* could go her way, and he reluctantly transshipped and headed south. On board, the crew set to the job of furling, and had the engine going in short order. Toward evening they sighted a few of the belated Bermuda racers who were also trapped on the polished surface of the windless sea.

As darkness approached, the captain paced the quarterdeck deep in a mood of vague uneasiness, as if he had sailed from Bermuda leaving something undone. Walking aft, he ran his eyes over the rigging aloft. The ship was neat and taut, no Irish pennants, no yards cockbill; everything in apple-pie order.

Then he looked skyward. A thin veil of cirrus clouds was dimming the twinkling stars. Before, they had been unusually bright. Suddenly the seasoned mariner had a chill feeling—something about the weather was simply not right.

A check showed the ship's barometer was behaving in peculiar fashion. The captain studied the sky again and was soon convinced that bad weather signs were there for the reading. He remembered seeing a faintly outlined fan-like cirrus formation in the west just before sunset and wondered if an undetected tropical disturbance lay at its base. Most likely it did.

The executive officer, who also served as navigator, was called on deck.

"How's the weather look to you?" the captain queried.

"All right, cap'n. If this breeze holds, we ought to make New York day after tomorrow morning."

"I hope you're right," the skipper responded, "but somehow I feel there is something fishy going on. I can't put my finger on it precisely, but I have the feeling we're going to get a dusting between here and New York."

Together the two officers reviewed the radio weather messages and the ship's barographic weather records from the previous several days. Adding up the information, the captain began to feel very pessimistic about the future conditions.

His first inclination was to change course then and there, heading due west. If there was anything foul in that direction, it would probably drift up to the northeastward and the *Eagle* could move in behind it.

But it had been months since the Americans had been home, and the captain reasoned that if any bad weather lay west of them, they would have heard about it in Bermuda.

Too, the gentle breeze had freshened and then held steady. Coming from the southeast, it was carrying the ship merrily along a direct course for home. As minutes passed into hours, the barometer steadied and the *Eagle* was snugged down for the night at sea.

By midnight, the captain decided to turn in. Taking a last look around, he noticed that the overlay of cirrus clouds above had thickened, and the stars were barely visible. The breeze and the barometer continued reassuringly without change, however, so he finally went to his cabin for some sleep.

Suddenly everything and everyone on the *Eagle* was wide awake!

With an abrupt lunge, every man below decks became aware of a sharp change topside. The soft monotone of the steady breeze had gone. In its place was a gusty, uneven moaning of wind—lots of wind! The *Eagle* was lurching through the dark in an uneasy fashion, as though in a resentful mood. In the blood-red glow of the night lights below, men were already scurrying about, squinting at each other through sleepy eyes opened too quickly. It must have been three or four in the morning.

Commander McGowan hurried onto the quarterdeck to have a look. The air felt wet and sticky. Groping forward through the dense humid darkness to the steering station, he could see the officer-of-the-deck and helmsmen silhouetted by the pale yellow radiance of the binnacle. Green haze fanning out from the starboard running light indicated that the air was saturated with moisture. The temperature had risen sharply, and the burbling wind, which the evening before had been a cool refreshing breeze, was now the fetid breath of bad weather.

Later, in the gray of coming light, low flying clouds scudded in from the east, and short showers of fine rain swept over the ship. At first they were barely noticeable, more like spray or mist than rain. But by dawn the barometer announced the bad news. With its needle plunging downward, it warned that the *Eagle* was in for a nasty blow.

As sunrise approached, the thickening overcast absorbed

the growing light, leaving the ship in a pre-dawn gloom. The spitting rain squalls gradually increased in frequency and intensity, while squally puffs of wind, each a little stronger than the one before, began to veer, hauling and backing as much as two points. One thing became certain. Commander Mc-Gowan and his *Eagle* were just ahead of a real hurricane.

Sizing up the situation, the captain recalled that in years past the most successful skippers of square-riggers had been those who had dared to drive a ship, and that many times the safety of the vessel, paradoxically, lay in the captain's daring to keep sail on when conservatism dictated that it should come off. He chose to keep on the sails set during the previous evening—the upper and lower foretopsails, the upper and lower main topsails and the fore and main courses. Those sails were made of the heaviest canvas and could be expected to stand a lot of wind. He chose, too, to run before the weather, bearing as much as possible to the westward. If they were truly in a tropical storm system, his earlier seaman's estimate of where the center lay should prove correct, and a westwardly course would keep the ship clear of the eye.

During the eight-to-noon watch Commander McGowan relieved the officer-of-the-deck and personally began conning the ship. The executive officer had been busily directing the storm preparations and was grateful to have an additional officer to help with the deck work. All hands were engaged in putting extra lashings on the boats, rigging lifelines, securing air ports, dogging down hatches and closing watertight doors. By mid-morning the *Eagle* was as secure as the crew could make her.

And none too soon. The mounting crescendo of wind, the thickening rain squalls, the rapidly building sea and the nose-diving barometer predicted that the weather would get much worse before it got better. Running before it, the *Eagle* no longer steered a course. Her heading was determined by wind direction alone—the captain trying to keep it nearly astern and off the starboard quarter. As long as the wind stayed in that direction, it would take the ship toward the New Jersey coast, and hopefully, out of the devilish weather.

The captain's frequent glances at the compass were just for the purposes of keeping informed of the *Eagle*'s heading. Until the navigator could get a sight of sun or stars, the ship's position between Bermuda and New York was strictly guess-work.

By noon the ocean's whitecaps had long since disappeared and been replaced by angry streaks gouged on the breasts of

Teamwork is the key to handling Eagle's *sails.*

waves by the clawing wind. Puffs had become roaring blasts as the average velocity rose above 50 knots. Soon even the streaks on the surface vanished, giving way to clouds of spray as wavetops were sheared off by the wind.

At that point, as every experienced mariner knew it would, the big sea began to build. With the beginning of the huge swells, the wind accelerated sharply until it was averaging about 60 knots. The barometric pressure continued to fall.

As the *Eagle* began to plunge and wallow, the men working on deck found it hard to retain their footing. Lest they be washed overboard, all hands were directed to remain where they were until further notice from the captain. There would be no relieving of the watches except for the relays of eight men at a time on the helm. Even with that number of willing hands trying to control the thrashing wheel, each team tired rapidly and had to be relieved at intervals of 15 to 20 minutes.

The storm drew closer; the tonal range of the wind was almost unbelievable. The earlier skirling and piping of the fresh gale through the rigging had risen in volume and in tone to bellowing and shrieking. The vastness of the sound seemed to fill the world. Shouted commands could no longer be understood, and the voices of the men died away and became inaudible. There, pressed against the eardrums, was sound without sound.

Each time the ship was overtaken by the massive sea her stern rose high in the air. As the wave moved forward, the stern would begin to settle back of the wave and momentarily the vessel would be suspended at her midship point with bow and stern protruding, each from its own side of the watery ridge. At that very moment, tons of green water would plunge in from port and starboard, filling the well-deck with brine and foam.

The mountainous sea was well developed, and each advancing face seemed almost vertical.

The wind, too, grew to a maddening ferocity and backed from northeast to north. Reading the ship's instruments, Commander McGowan learned that she was crashing along at 16 knots—faster than the *Horst Wessel* had ever sailed! A messenger brought word to the quarter deck that the anemometer needle was at the top of the scale. The wind velocity had gone beyond 80 knots!

Almost instantly, the voice of the storm was more than a roar. There was added a sharp sound of tearing—a ripping of the fabric of the very Gates of Hell. Bellowing blasts, born of the tropical heat and slowly accumulated during the months of brooding at the edge of the doldrums, were the main theme.

The fore upper and lower topsails were the first to go. One moment they were there; a second later they had vanished into the Niagara of spray. From the yards, ragged little ribbons fluttered where a broad expanse of sail had just been drawing. With the next gust, the foresail and main upper topsail blew out, but the mainsail and main lower topsail still held. The *Eagle*'s speed slackened, but only slightly.

With some of her sails in shreds and her decks pounded by the still increasing sea and wind, the *Eagle* had begun to dive and wallow like a wild, wounded thing. With every new wave the captain looked more apprehensively astern. He could continue to sail downwind and risk the chance of having the following sea break over the stern and sweep forward across the poop deck, probably tearing away everything in its way. Or, he could heave to, hoping to ride the tempest out.

There was grave danger in either action, and Commander McGowan knew it. To reach the hove-to position, the *Eagle* would have to be turned through an angle of more than 90 degrees. That would allow her to have wind and seas coming in from the direction slightly forward of the beam. But such a maneuver would present the threat of broaching and having the ship go over on her beam end. If the *Eagle* broached, it would be the last of everyone on board.

As though things weren't bad enough, the ship received a message from an American freighter: URGENT TO ALL SHIPS —AM IN LATITUDE 37–30 N, LONGITUDE 72–30 W—UNABLE TO MANEUVER IN HEAVY WIND AND SEA—ALL VESSELS PLEASE KEEP CLEAR, MASTER. The *Eagle*'s radio operator had scribbled at the bottom of the dispatch: "Loud signal— sounds close."

"Poor devil," Commander McGowan thought. "That skipper must have sent his message out to bolster his own morale. It could not serve any other purpose."

Visibility on the *Eagle* had been reduced to only a few yards. If the floundering merchantman should suddenly loom up out of the murk ahead, there would not be a chance in the world of avoiding a collision. Both ships would go down.

The captain briefly thought of the futility of abandoning ship in that sea, should the worst occur. It was simply impossible. No smallboat could live, even if it should be lucky enough to get away from the ship's side without being dashed to pieces. The *Eagle* was committed to hanging on right where she was and making the best of it.

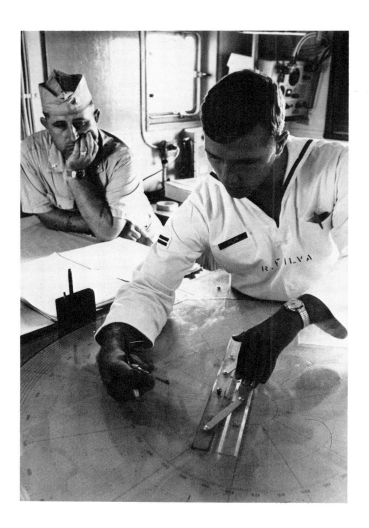

A cadet learns the dangers of sailing near other ships.

The next sea forced a command decision. It was the largest of all and crashed down on the *Eagle* with shattering immensity, catching her at a slight angle. That was just what the captain had been trying so desperately to avoid. With her entire hull quivering, the ship partially broached, then literally dove into the ocean. The bowsprit and entire forecastle disappeared under green water all the way to the base of the foremast.

The mainsail billowed like a child's balloon and exploded. The *Eagle* rolled deeply to starboard, hanging for a heart-stopping moment at the bottom of the roll. While every man on deck clung to rail or lifeline, the captain stared across the quarterdeck almost straight down into the boiling surface of the sea.

The water that had been scooped up by the forecastle went thundering aft, burying everything under a foamy burden as the *Eagle* fought her way upright with laboring effort. She couldn't stand many repetitions of that.

Immediately after another wave, the helmsmen were ordered to put the wheel over to left full rudder. At the same time the ship's engine, which had been brought on the line earlier, was set at two-thirds ahead. As the ship's bow began to swing, the engine was stopped, and it seemed that everyone on board started to pray. The next 30 seconds were critical.

The men on the braces and those on the mizzensails sensed the dangerous situation and worked with desperate haste. The ship snapped around to her new heading as though mounted on a pivot. The yards were braced around and the mizzensail carried into place to balance the foresails as the vessel moved up on the wind.

As the first sea bore down on the *Eagle,* the towering cliff face of water appeared higher than the masts. It seemed impossible that the ship could survive the climb up the precipice. At once, the roller-coaster ride began, but she remained steady as a church.

Under the new pressure of the wind the *Eagle* heeled to starboard about 20 degrees, but the wild confusion was over. With their sharp angle to the continuing gusts, the sails began to draw, causing the vessel to feel her rudder and head slightly more to windward. With a change in direction the sails began to spill, the ship lost headway and canceled her rudder action. This steadying cycle continued about every five minutes.

The *Eagle* was in a position where she rode most easily in relation to sea and wind. Her survival was now out of the skipper's hands and would be decided by fate and

her designers. Hove to, the captain and crew became observers.

By three in the afternoon the *Eagle*'s barometer showed the first signs of her victory. The pressure was rising almost as fast as it had fallen some eight hours before. Together with a gradual wind shift to the northwest, it told everyone that the storm was dying. As evening approached, the recovery was rapid.

Commander McGowan and his officers went about the ship inspecting the damage. In just a few hectic moments, $20,000 worth of sails had gone with the wind. The tattered remains gave the *Eagle* a raffish air. But no other damage was major. By some great stroke of luck not a man had been lost or injured.

Those who were new to the sea and to square-riggers had taken their first test in the highest order of seamanship and were still on their feet. As they went about putting their ship back in order, Commander McGowan felt a surge of satisfaction with the *Eagle* and her crew. Their initiation had been a severe one.

By sunset the sky had cleared. The storm was over. Before dark the sea settled down and the *Eagle* resumed her journey.

The next morning, she arrived at home.

The usual summer haze had lifted from Long Island Sound, and the ebbing tide was washing over Bartlett Reef and off the sandy shores of Ocean Beach. The breaking sun sparkled on the Thames River, reflecting the red roofs and white-clapboarded houses of New London. For a sleepy Sunday morning in June, the townspeople already seemed to be up and about the waterfront. On a corner of Whalers Row, a boy stood selling *The New York Times* from the back of his toy wagon. A few scattered yachts drifting between the shore and Ledge Light carried summer sailors eagerly awaiting the day's first good breeze.

High on a bluff overlooking the Thames, the ivy-covered brick buildings of the United States Coast Guard Academy basked in warming sunshine. Amid a green hillside lawn behind Hamilton Hall, wooden bleachers, now empty, and a solitary speakers' platform were all that remained of the starched white uniforms, the martial music and proud voices of yesterday's graduation ceremonies. Another class of Coast Guard officers, all bright and polished, had gone to distant assignments.

In the Academy's quay on the river, the *Eagle,* fresh from winter months in a Maryland shipyard, lay straining against her lines. Soon she would be free of them.

There was a bustle of activity on her decks as cadets stowed gear, made up lines and prepared every piece of equipment for sea. This was sailing day! Very soon the *Eagle* and her crew would be away, bound on a voyage across the Atlantic to Europe.

Just after nine o'clock, lines were taken in or cast off; the *Eagle* swung away from the Academy dock and moved out into Thames Channel under the high New London Bridge and into the lower harbor. There she anchored to step both of her topgallant masts, which had been lowered for the bridge. For the remainder of the day she anchored in the same bay from which fast clippers and Yankee whaleships had once sailed round the world. That gave the cadets a brief chance to settle in for sea.

'Tweendecks, nearly 200 young men would live together during the cruise. The upper classmen would sleep in the pipe cots tiered on the starboard side, aft. The under classmen, much like early American sailors on the frigate *Constitution,* would doze in hammocks slung in the rest of the area. Each cadet was assigned a locker in which to hang his uniforms, and perhaps later, to stow souvenirs. They would all eat at mess tables in the same 'tweendecks, since their hammocks

Eagle at her berth at the Coast Guard Academy, New London, Connecticut.

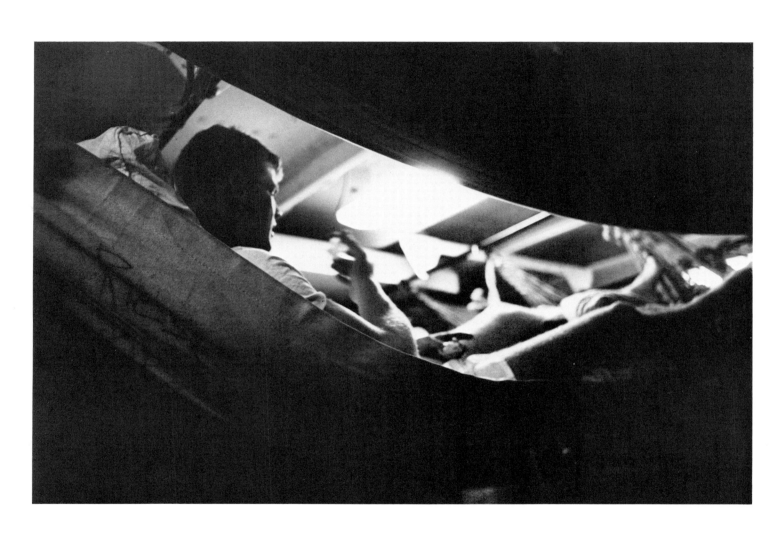

*Above: Some cadets sleep in
hammocks 'tween decks.
Right: Down comes a staysail
as the wind takes a holiday.*

would daily be consigned to large bins along the bulkheads.

The following day was marked by a shake-down run on Long Island Sound, the great bark tacking and reaching in the blue waters west and south of Fishers Island. It was a pleasant day with steady breezes, giving the cadets a few final sail-drills before the real thing. The captain put the big ship through her paces while officers and cadets alike gained the feel of their ship. At nightfall, she returned to her anchorage once more.

"Loose the tops'ls!" "Man the sheets!" "Throw off the buntlines and ease the clews!" "Sheet home and belay!" The orders rang out in the morning air fore and aft. Standing on the quarterdeck, a young cadet held a red megaphone to his lips and called. From the fore and main masts, cadet mast captains echoed and relayed each signal. Aloft, chain sheets rattled and clanged on the steel yards as white-uniformed youths unleashed all sails.

In moments, tall pyramids of shapely canvas piled high above the teak decks and slowly, then more rapidly, the *Eagle* moved off to seaward passing south of Block Island and leaving Long Island's Montauk Point to the west. Aft, the cadet officer-of-the-watch—a fellow from Iowa—walked the bleached poop, his eyes glancing at the cadets on the helm, the cadet boatswains, navigators, quartermasters. Leaning against the weather rail, a young commissioned officer unobtrusively watched the proceedings; but the responsibility of the deck was the cadet's as far as that was humanly possible and desirable.

The wind was quiet at first, and the ship scudded along at about four knots, her masts upright and the decks all steady, almost as if she were not moving at all. At the end of the high gaff, Old Glory fluttered in the easy breeze.

As the *Eagle*'s cutwater cleft through the first long Atlantic swells, a white Coast Guard cutter, steaming along merrily, took her station well off the starboard quarter. There she would remain for the entire cruise, escorting the bark and sometimes exchanging a few upper classmen with her. On board the cutter, those men would learn the workings of a modern Coast Guard ship at sea.

Before setting sail from New London, the captain and his officers had carefully charted the route for the entire cruise. The *Eagle* would sail south toward Ambrose Lightship off New York and then veer due east at about Latitude 40, roughly paralleling in a reverse direction the course of Columbus. North of the Azores, she would head toward the Bay

of Biscay, making her first European port-of-call at Santander, Spain.

From Santander, the ship would go north through the English Channel and the Strait of Dover to Amsterdam, followed by a crossing of the North Sea to Copenhagen.

The homeward voyage would duplicate the route sailed by the Vikings when they set out for Greenland and the fabled Vinland.

Now the *Eagle* was on her way. The crossing to Spain would take about 20 days—days filled with adventure and with learning.

Although the *Eagle* has no classrooms on board, she is first of all a school ship, designed to train young men for the demanding duties of Coast Guard commissioned officers. Each cruise is intended essentially for practical work. Instruction is in the open, on deck, and the ship herself provides a good deal of it. Every day, after the midday muster, the captain devises some imaginary calamity or accident which the cadets must deal with at once. There are exercises of all sorts: man overboard, fire and collision, sail handling and maneuvering the ship.

Life on board the *Eagle* is organized so that the cadets handle the big square-rigger themselves, tacking her and bringing her to, getting away the small boats, and manipulating her sails to take best advantage of the wind.

As far as can be arranged, each young man has a chance to learn all the jobs both on deck and below. The upper classmen, having sailed the ship before, provide the leadership and fill the key billets on the watches. The under classmen are entrusted with less exacting tasks. And always there are the officers, watching and evaluating.

Sometimes, the handsome windjammer finds herself going through rather odd contortions, and there is, at times, a lack of precision to the maneuvers. But only momentarily does it matter. Absolute perfection is not the point. The point is that the cadets are doing the job—doing and learning, all the time.

On Sunday, there is church, held on deck when possible—always with Protestant, Catholic and Jewish services. Against the backdrop of sea and sails, these are often profoundly moving.

There are leisure diversions, too, in the little time allowed to enjoy them. Movies or "homegrown" music or an amateur skit fills the evenings. Occasionally, there is also a contest or joking game.

On this voyage, as on most, days soon faded into weeks as the *Eagle* sailed on toward Spain, sometimes with fine sunshine and brisk winds, more often with bad wind and no sun at all. At times she had to beat to windward, cutting this way and then that, zigzagging across the North Atlantic, and the faithful cutter zigzagged along behind her.

On the whole, however, the *Eagle*'s progress was very good, for she often came up to 15 knots and made little fuss about it. With the wind singing in her efficient rigging, her deep sails would fill and draw, pushing her through the white-capped sea like a racer.

"Here is a good ship for Cape Horn!" Captain Alan Villiers, himself a square-riggerman and school-ship master, had once said of the *Eagle*. "She could carry the Stars and Stripes anywhere."

With all sail set, the *Eagle* can stand up in a 30-knot blow. Between New York and the coast of Europe, she has done it more than once.

On one particular night, though—her log recorded that she was just northwest of the Azores—the high-flying royals were made fast in a howling squall. The rain was driving and the wind growling through the rigging. The white bark lay over, streaking through the rising sea like a midnight phantom. Salt sprays clouded the forecastle, dashing up and around the headsails.

The order was given, "Clew up the fore royal!" This was classic stuff from the days of Donald McKay's great clippers. Clewlines and buntlines were manned and thrown off belaying pins.

"Lower away! Haul away on those clewlines, there! Round in the lee brace!"

Down went the thrashing royal, smothered in its own gear. Aloft climbed four cadets, hanging to the weather ratlines. In short order, the flapping canvas was secure in its gaskets. Aft, the rest of the watch was already taking in the main royal the same way.

There were four men on the wheel now, and the captain had come on the quarterdeck, but he was quietly, patiently, leaving everything to the cadets. He knew that the feeling of responsibility was worthless unless it could be exercised in foul as well as good times.

The cadets on the mainmast fought their way to the uppermost yard and were having the ride of their lives. As the *Eagle* rolled, these cadets were first out over the boiling deep, when she rolled back again, they were perched high above the

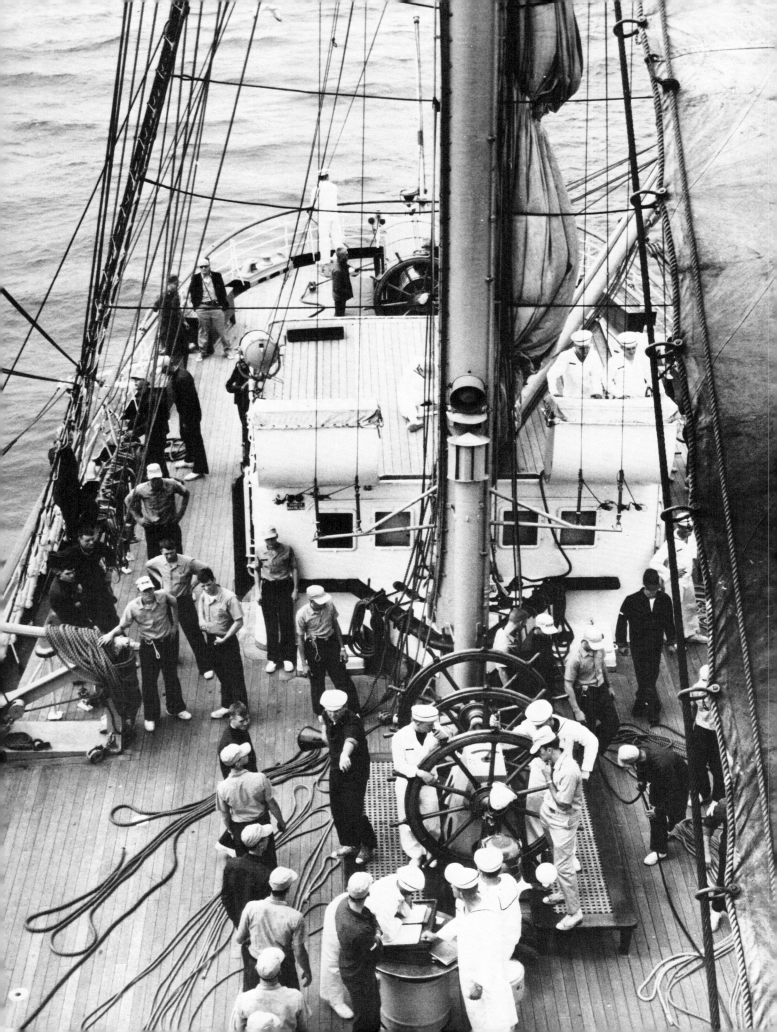

decks. The wet and wind-stiffened sail puffed out, then threatened to blow back over them. Streaming with rain, but paying little attention to all the motion, they wrestled with the fighting-mad sail. Soon they had it rolled neatly up along the yard.

With the increasing sea more canvas whipped in the night as fathoms of nylon line ran through well-kept blocks and other sails were taken in. The flying jib, the three-cornered gaff topsail, the royal staysails—all were doused by excited cadets, glad to have a crack at such thrilling work.

Later, scuttlebutt had it that two senior officers were also aloft. The story, so it went, was that a four-striped captain and a full commander had gone up just for the fun of it!

Crossing the Atlantic in the 40 latitudes, the *Eagle* sailed a lonely road. Most ships eastbound turned north at about Longitude 50 West and headed for the English Channel ports. But the *Eagle* had stayed on a course straight for Spain, and she encountered remarkably few other seafarers. Once, a few days beyond Long Island, a huge Cunard liner was spotted on the northern horizon, and that same day the bark was overhauled by an American freighter bound for the Mediterranean. Briefly sailing along together, the two ships made an odd contrast. Then each dipped its colors in the usual maritime courtesy and sailed on its way. No other ships were sighted until the *Eagle* was off the coast of Europe.

For most of the under classmen, Santander was their first glimpse of Europe. It was a clean and gracious port surrounded by the picturesque Spanish countryside. The tile and stucco village served as a good introduction to the colorful past and handsome present of that land. Of special interest was its centuries-old connection with the sea trade to the Americas. Seamen from there had shipped out with Columbus, and the streets still reflected the past riches brought back by early trading galleons.

Ample shore leave for the cadets, in turn, allowed them to see as much of the country as possible. They had worked hard at sea—very hard—and now in port, it was time to relax.

For five days they enjoyed side trips to Altamira, where ancients had left rock paintings 20,000 years before; to Santanillo and Cabo Mayor, and to the Royal Palace, where Spanish monarchs once summered. There were also parties and receptions on board the *Eagle* and ashore, and a few times the revelry lasted on toward dawn.

The Spanish hospitality was so inviting and so abundant that even the liveliest among the *Eagle*'s crew were pleased at last to go to sea again. Although there was minimum time for sleeping on board, at least it was regular and more or less predictable.

Leaving Santander, the *Eagle* romped briskly across the Bay of Biscay and headed up the English Channel for her next port of call, Amsterdam. Spared the legendary Biscay storms, that passage was interesting and by no means difficult. In the shipping lanes of Europe, coastal packets rivaled with huge oil tankers showing flags of far-off lands for a chance to salute the shapely sailing ship. The *Eagle* was doing a great job of showing the flag, though that was not her purpose.

At Amsterdam, the *Eagle* docked almost among the green trees, her long bowsprit standing over the waterfront traffic like a clipper of old along New York's South Street. She had scarcely tied up before a young naval officer was aboard welcoming the cadets to the Netherlands and offering them a variety of sightseeing and entertainment which soon beckoned them ashore.

For another five days there was pleasant shore-going: visits to diamond cutters, trips to aroma-filled cheese markets and colorful flower gardens, excursions through the city's canals on tour boats, and a cordial exchange of social affairs.

Many of the cadets hired bicycles or scooters for visits to the dike-guarded farms and villages of the interior, while others spent time admiring the priceless Rembrandts in the Rijks Museum. A few with relatives in other countries were allowed brief trips to Germany or to Belgium, France and England.

It was extraordinary how fast time passed for the cadets during their calls ashore. In just a few great experiences, the five days at Amsterdam were gone and it was time for the *Eagle* to be off again.

By way of the North Sea Canal, the ship soon entered the fishing port of IJmuiden and then passed out into the North Sea itself.

There was a week at sea between Amsterdam and the next port, Copenhagen, but if time flew past in port, it also went quickly at sea. It was early July, and for once the North Sea was in a quiet mood. On a sunny afternoon the coast of Norway came up on the horizon and off its banks, a host of little fishing craft and tiny coasters darted about. Within hours the white bark approached the confined waters between Sweden and Denmark. Reluctantly, the *Eagle*'s sails were furled and her little-used diesel engine was put to work. She sailed down through the Skagerrak and, just off Elsinore, passed the lovely Danish full-rigged ship *Danmark*.

*Opposite: A visit with Dutch
farmers on Marken Island.
Above: Like a clipper along
old New York's South Street,*
Eagle *points her bowsprit
over traffic in Amsterdam.*

Entering the clean, ship-filled harbor at Copenhagen, the *Eagle* was given a berth along the Langelinie, the most desirable spot on the long waterfront. Nearby, Hans Christian Andersen's famous Little Mermaid turned her fairytale gaze toward the sea, and the tree-lined and fountain-decorated streets twisted toward the twilighted city.

In Copenhagen, the good Danes provided more entertainment, more sightseeing and more friendships. Amid Tivoli's famous gardens, the twinkling lights and summer music provided a setting romantic enough for any seaman just come ashore, and the cadets were quick to make the best of it.

During the days, tours were made of Hamlet's castle at Elsinore, the Danish version of Times Square—beloved Raadhuspladsen—and the marine museum at Kronborg. The cadets gazed with fascination at scale models of old Danish merchantmen and training ships like the full-rigged *Georg Stage* and fabulous five-masted *Kjobenhaven,* which years before had been tragically lost with all hands.

The museum director told the cadets, "She was the best sailing ship in all the world when she set sail from Montevideo one day in '28, but the sea took her just the same. And nothing whatever has been seen or heard of her since."

For some of the cadets that thought lingered the rest of their visit in Copenhagen. It was a haunting one, especially since they, too, were living under sail at sea.

In a few short days July passed its mid-point, and the time arrived for the *Eagle* to leave European waters. She was scheduled to be back in New London by the second week in August to take the second and fourth classmen on a short cruise to Bermuda. Without delay, the officers and cadets secured their ship for sea, and using the spankers to swing her short in Ore Sound, sailed away from Copenhagen. Outside the point of Elsinore, the full-rigged *Danmark* was met under sail, and the two square-riggers sailed along together, presenting a majestic sight rarely seen in modern days. It was a heart-warming interlude, and the cadets on the *Eagle* were delighted to have a chance to show their windjamming skills among such veterans.

Ahead lay 3,600 nautical miles of the open North Atlantic. The route she sailed would take her close to Iceland, Greenland and Newfoundland, but her voyage did not include ports-of-call at any place.

It was a route first plied by the Danish and the Norwegian Vikings. Mariners down the years have held that east winds blew there carrying any ship swiftly across the cold gray

waters. This year they did not. For 26 days the *Eagle* slogged to windward with seldom a let-up in the bad weather or a peaceful moment on the sullen, ill-tempered Atlantic.

Still, her captain was determined, knowing that his cadets were cut from something very tough—an experience and will that made them seadogs all.

At exactly four bells on the morning of August 13, the *Eagle* dropped anchor again in New London. She was one day ahead of schedule.

To fully appreciate the beauty of *Eagle* sailing and understand the traditions of mastering the sea under sail, the cadets must first know their ship, her gear, and her temperament in all kinds of weather. They must learn these early in their Academy careers, and long before they are required to put this knowledge into practice.

Many of the names and actions used on the *Eagle* have deep roots in the lore of men going down to the sea in square-rigged sailing ships.

The 295-foot *Eagle* is built of German steel on the transverse framing system. When this vessel was built, the fully-welded technique had not yet been developed. In general, the seams are riveted and the butts are welded. Fittings are bolted on, while strength members such as knees and gussets are welded to the frames. The plating is of approximately 4/10-inch thickness.

With her beam of about 40 feet and a 17-foot draft, she has two full-length steel decks, a platform deck below these, and a raised forecastle and quarterdeck. The weather decks have three inches of teak laid on top of the steel. The second deck has a three-inch pine layer covered with vinyl tile. The platform deck and the tank tops are steel.

The second deck is the damage control deck. There are six watertight bulkheads which run to the main deck but which have watertight doors on the second—or living—deck level. The main deck under the forecastle contains the paint locker, washrooms, and heads. Enlisted crew's quarters are forward on the second deck followed by two large compartments which are the cadet quarters. Aft of this, under the quarterdeck, are the officers' quarters. Under the crew's quarters are commissary holds and refrigerator spaces. Under the forward cadet quarters on this hold deck are stowage spaces, carpenter's shop and sailmaker's shop. Below this platform deck are the water and fuel tanks. Under the after cadet quarters are the engine room spaces. Under the officers' quarters, aft, are miscellaneous storerooms. The galley is on the main deck abaft the forecastle, and the cadet berthing compartments double as messing compartments.

The lower masts, topmasts, the topgallant masts, the royal masts, bowsprit, yards, booms, and mizzen gaff on the *Eagle* are all made of hollow steel tubes. All of these various appurtenances of the ship are known as spars. The foremast is stepped on the second deck, the mainmast is stepped on the keel and the mizzenmast is stepped on the platform deck over the engine shaft alley. The fore and main masts, together with

their yards, are identical.

The *Eagle* follows the rigging practices of large sailing ships at their final stage of development. The foremast and its topmast are really one hollow tube, as is the mainmast and its topmast. However, they are rigged as the older vessels were with shrouds that come in under the tops, where a new system of topmast shrouds originates. The two parts of the masts retain their original names, that is, foremast from the deck to the top and foretopmast from the top to the crosstrees. The same applies to the main.

Aboard the *Eagle,* the yards and other spars take the names of the masts to which they are attached and, logically enough, each shroud, backstay, and stay takes the name of the mast which it supports. The sails take the names of the yards or stays on which they are set.

The running rigging is what really contributes density to the apparent maze of gear aloft. However, the cadets soon learn that each sail is controlled by certain lines, some of which are used to set the sail, some to trim it, and others to furl it. The clews, or lower corners, of a squaresail must be held down. This is done by lines known as sheets. On the upper sails these sheets run to the yardarm below. On the lower sails the sheets run directly to the hull. When the sails are set on the wind, another line called the weather tack holds the forward clew of the sail and the lee sheet holds the other clew down and aft. The yards are swung by lines known as braces. Each brace takes the name of the yard it controls and may be called by starboard and port or by lee and weather as circumstances direct. The yards are held level or canted by means of lines known as lifts. These lifts are likewise known as starboard and port or lee and weather and by the names of the yard to which they are attached.

Sails are furled by cadets on deck using clewlines, leechlines, and buntlines. The clewlines work opposite the sheets and are used to haul the clews, or corners, of the sails up to the yards. The leechlines haul the sides, or leeches, of the sails up to the yards and the buntlines haul the middle and foot up to the yards.

Halyards are the most important pieces of running gear. Each halyard takes the name of the yard it hauls aloft. Generally speaking, the sails are set by letting go and overhauling the buntlines and leechlines, easing down clewlines, hauling down the sheets, and hoisting up the yard by means of the halyard. They are furled by lowering the yard, and by hauling up the sail with the clewlines, buntlines, and leech-

SPARS AND STANDING RIGGING

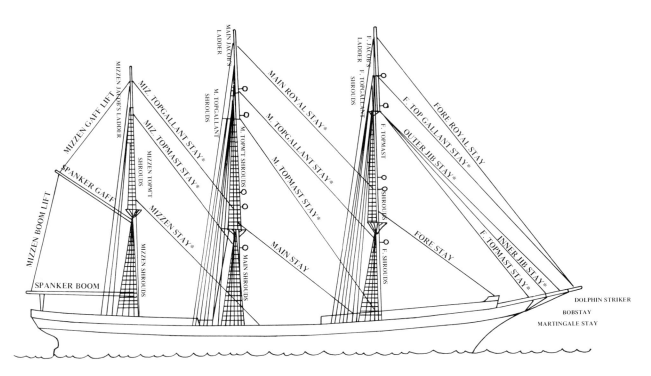

1. Stays which are marked with an asterisk carry staysails or headsails.
2. Backstays, like headstays, are named for the part of the mast from which they lead.
3. Moveable yards (upper topsails, topgallants, and royals) are shown in their down positions.
4. Fore and main topgallant masts can be "housed" to reduce masthead height.

STANDING RIGGING

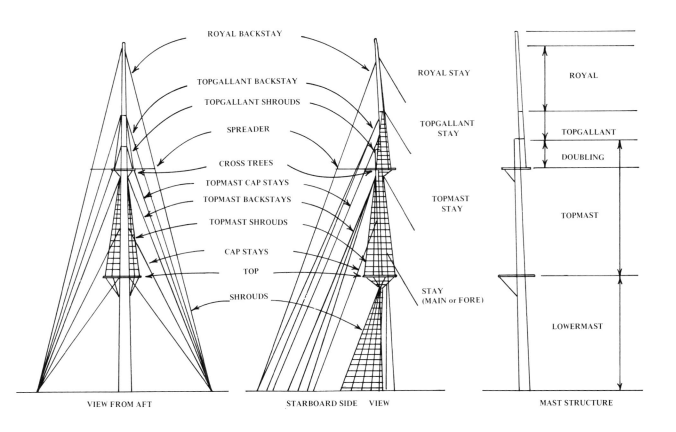

lines. Thus, 90 per cent of the work of setting and furling the sails can be done from the ship's deck.

The beauty and power of the *Eagle* lie in her ten squaresails. Those on the foremast are exactly like those on the mainmast.

The top edge—or head—of each squaresail is attached to a yard. The sail takes the name of the yard to which it is attached and is below this yard when it is set.

The mainsail and lower topsail are set from "fixed" or "standing" yards. These yards do move, but are so called because they do not slide up or down the mast as others do. Under most weather conditions these two sails are quite simple to set. Essentially, they are dropped from the yard and the two lower corners controlled or attached to keep the sail from slatting about and to make the sail draw.

On the command "Let fall!" the sail is pushed off the forward side of the yard. This command may be given by the cadet mast captain or he may have directed the cadet yard captain to give it. Once the sail is pushed off the yard, the yardmen move in to the mast. Two cadets remain in at the mast and overhaul the buntlines and leechlines as needed. After having been pushed off the yard, the sail is called "in its gear." Once the cadets are off the yard, and at the cadet mast captain's command, the buntlines and leechlines are thrown off their belaying pins and are allowed to run freely. The clewlines are eased smartly and the sail is sheeted home. Normally, the cadets find it necessary to haul taut the weather tack and the lee sheet to make the mainsail set properly.

Essentially what has been said for the courses and lower topsails applies to the remaining three squaresails—with some additions. The additions are necessary because the upper three yards move up and down their masts on tracks.

In setting a sail from a movable yard, it is loosed, let fall, and sheeted home. In addition, the cadets must hoist the yard aloft. The sheets for the next sail aloft are thrown off, the buntlines, bunt-leechlines and/or leechlines are thrown off, the clewlines eased, the sheets hauled home, and the halyard hauled smartly. The final stage of hoisting the yard is accomplished slowly and is done hand-over-hand. Just enough strain is brought on the leeches of the sail to make them set taut.

Squaresails on the *Eagle* are set in the following order: lower topsail, upper topsail, mainsail or foresail, topgallant sail, royal sail. These squaresails are taken in and furled in the reverse order of setting. The mainsail and the lower topsail are usually easy to set and to furl. Essentially, the reverse procedure of setting is used by the cadets to furl the square-sails. Buntlines, leechlines, and clewlines are manned, and sheets (tacks also for the mainsail) are tended. The sheets and tacks are eased smartly and the sail is hoisted up to the yard by the buntlines, leechlines and clewlines. On command, the cadets lay aloft and furl the sail. They often start aloft before the sail is up in its gear in order to get out and start furling just as soon as possible. The first cadets always go out on the weather yardarm and start smothering canvas.

The *Eagle* has four headsails and six staysails. All are similar in shape and operation.

In general, each staysail and headsail has a halyard, a downhaul, and a sheet. Headsails have two sheets. The halyard and the downhaul oppose one another, as their purpose is opposite. They remain rigged all the time. Sheets for the headsails remain rigged and on their respective sides of the forecastle. Sheets for the staysails are stowed in the crosstrees, in the tops, or on deck and must be rigged on the proper side each time the sail is set.

For setting these sails the gaskets securing the furled sail are cleared away and the sheet rigged and led free on the lee side. The downhaul is laid out free for running and is tended by one cadet. The halyard and sheet are manned. The halyard is hauled smartly and the downhaul is allowed to run freely. A light strain is taken on the sheet to keep the sail from slatting about and tearing itself apart. When the sail is nearly close-up, the halyard is hauled hand-over-hand to insure that an abrupt and severe strain does not come on the boltrope. When the halyard is belayed, the sheet is trimmed. Since a square-rigged vessel cannot lie as close to the wind as a fore-and-aft ship, the staysails on the *Eagle* are never trimmed in tight.

As with the squaresails, the reverse procedure of setting is used in taking in and furling the staysails and headsails.

The spanker is a large gaff-headed sail that sets from the mizzenmast. It provides a drawing or driving power for the *Eagle,* but often it is more important for its balancing effect and help in steering. Located well aft of the pivot point of the vessel, it has a considerable moment.

In setting the spanker, the spanker boom is hauled to the appropriate side depending on the tack being sailed. The boom is then topped up by the use of the topping lift. The weather vang is slacked as is the weather flag halyard. Radio transmitters are then lowered before cadets are sent aloft.

LIFTS AND BRACES

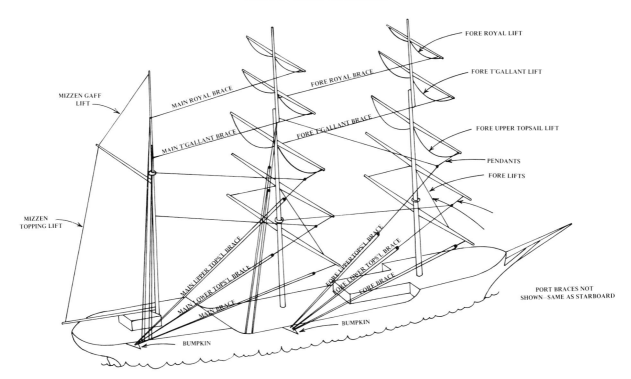

MIZZEN GAFF LIFT

MIZZEN TOPPING LIFT

MAIN ROYAL BRACE

FORE ROYAL BRACE

FORE ROYAL LIFT

FORE T'GALLANT LIFT

MAIN T'GALLANT BRACE

FORE T'GALLANT BRACE

FORE UPPER TOPSAIL LIFT

PENDANTS

FORE LIFTS

MAIN UPPER TOPS'L BRACE

MAIN LOWER TOPS'L BRACE

FORE UPPER TOPS'L BRACE

FORE LOWER TOPS'L BRACE

FORE BRACE

MAIN BRACE

MAIN BRACE

PORT BRACES NOT SHOWN—SAME AS STARBOARD

BUMPKIN

BUMPKIN

SAIL PLAN - USCGC EAGLE

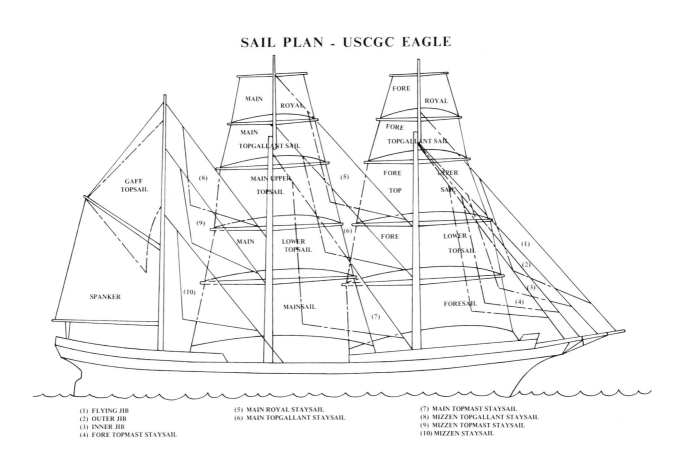

MAIN ROYAL

FORE ROYAL

MAIN TOPGALLANT SAIL

FORE TOPGALLANT SAIL

GAFF TOPSAIL

MAIN UPPER TOPSAIL

FORE UPPER TOPSAIL

MAIN LOWER TOPSAIL

FORE LOWER TOPSAIL

SPANKER

MAINSAIL

FORESAIL

(1) FLYING JIB
(2) OUTER JIB
(3) INNER JIB
(4) FORE TOPMAST STAYSAIL

(5) MAIN ROYAL STAYSAIL
(6) MAIN TOPGALLANT STAYSAIL

(7) MAIN TOPMAST STAYSAIL
(8) MIZZEN TOPGALLANT STAYSAIL
(9) MIZZEN TOPMAST STAYSAIL
(10) MIZZEN STAYSAIL

Classroom for cadets on deck.

The head and foot of the sail are hauled out until the scallops in the boltrope along the head and foot are removed.

Once the sail is set, it is sometimes necessary to ease the topping lift to insure the proper shape in the leech of the sail. The full weight of the boom is not borne by the sail so there is always a strain on the topping lift. Taking in and furling the spanker is almost the exact reverse of setting it.

The gaff topsail is very similar to a staysail. The sail has a halyard, a sheet, a clewline, and a tack.

In setting the gaff topsail, one or, at most, two cadets are sent aloft to clear away the gaskets and to lower the tack on the proper side. The halyard and sheet are manned and the clewline laid out clear for running. The clewline is allowed to run freely as the halyard and sheet are hauled home. Exactly the reverse procedure is used for taking in the sail.

Fore and aft sails on the *Eagle* are trimmed by their sheets. The closer to the wind the vessel is sailing, the further in these sails must be trimmed, yet they are trimmed only flat enough to remove the luffing from the sail. To balance the vessel, the headsails are sometimes trimmed a bit flatter. This may ease the mizzen staysails and spanker to the point where they are allowed to luff just the slightest bit. This is only done when sailing close hauled and is done to overcome the necessity of carrying rudder to keep the vessel on course.

The squaresails are trimmed by braces. The courses are also trimmed by sheets and tacks. When sailing as close to the wind as possible the yards are braced up so that the lee yardarm is just touching the backstays, but no strain is brought on the backstays. As the wind draws aft, the yards are braced in. When the wind is dead aft, the yards are braced square. When the *Eagle* is under power, the yards are always braced so that they present the least resistance to the wind.

Although a fore-and-aft-rigged vessel can generally sail within four or five points of the wind, a square-rigged vessel does well to sail within seven. One of the reasons for this is that the yards of a square-rigger can be braced up only about four points before they fetch up against the lee backstays. A fore-and-aft sail can be trimmed in much closer to the centerline of the ship.

When the *Eagle* enjoys winds which permit her to make good the desired course, it is necessary only to trim sail to best advantage and let her go.

Keeping the sails of the *Eagle* properly trimmed, however, is an art. An alert watch which pays close attention to trim can make as much as ten miles more than a watch which is careless in this regard. Thus, it is a point of pride with each cadet officer-of-the-deck to keep his sails trimmed to maximum advantage at all times. *In sailing ships, this is one of the hallmarks of competence.*

When the *Eagle* is sailing directly before the wind, the maximum propelling effect is realized by bracing the yards square and trimming them parallel to the horizon. Staysails and headsails do not draw; hence, they are normally down. Squaresails on the foremast are blanked to a considerable extent by those on the mainmast. To reduce this blanking effect the cadets "soft sheet" the mainsails or even take the main course up in its gear.

When the ship is sailing hard on the wind, the cadet officer-of-the-deck usually wants the yards braced up as far as they will go and still draw effectively. The extent to which the yards may be braced up is limited by the rigging. To have all sails drawing to maximum advantage generally requires a fan, i.e., the upper yards braced progressively further in than the lower ones. Fanned squaresails also give warning when the vessel is coming too close to the wind. The royals and topgallants, being braced in more than the topsails and the courses, start to lift before the topsails and courses. This warns the cadet officer-of-the-deck to fall off a bit. It allows a margin of steering error and reduces the likelihood of the ship accidentally being caught aback.

In addition to being properly braced, yardarms are properly trimmed, or kept parallel to the horizon. This is done by adjusting the lifts while easing or hauling on lee sheets and weather tacks, as necessary. Obviously, close attention by officers and cadets is required to keep the vessel sailing to maximum advantage when close hauled.

Since only fore-and-aft-rigged vessels can sail close on the wind, it is never necessary to trim *Eagle*'s headsails, staysails, and spanker flat. These sails should always be somewhat free when the squaresails are braced up sharp. In general, they are trimmed so they are just full.

When the *Eagle*'s desired course is upwind, and it often is, she can make progress only by sailing a series of "boards" or tacks. First with the wind on one side, then on the other, her progress in the desired direction becomes the sum of the components of the various boards in that direction.

Working the *Eagle* directly to windward in this fashion is an extremely slow and laborious process. During heavy weather little or no progress can be made. For this reason it is dangerous for any square-rigger to be "caught on a lee

One white light shows the Eagle *is at anchor.*

shore" in a storm. Fortunately, however, the wind is seldom directly opposite the course which must be made good, and reasonable progress can usually be made in the desired direction.

When it is necessary to maneuver to bring the wind from one side to the other, there are two basic ways of doing it: tacking and wearing. A third method, boxhauling, is a combination of the two. In tacking, the ship's bow is brought through the wind. In wearing, the ship's bow is turned away from the wind and the stern through it. In boxhauling, the ship's bow is initially thrown up into the wind, after which the vessel is backed around stern to wind, then sailed around on the other tack as in wearing.

Tacking is the usual method of coming about when beating to windward. Its advantages are that the vessel must swing through only about 12 points of the compass rather than 20, and that the ship generally continues to make some distance to windward during the maneuver. However, tacking is not feasible in very light or very heavy weather. The *Eagle* must be thrown up into the wind with all squaresails aback. This kills her headway very quickly. If she had little speed to start with, she will probably not go through the wind. Instead, she will fall back on the same tack. In very strong winds it is imprudent to attempt to tack. The masts and rigging of the *Eagle* are designed primarily for wind forces acting on the backsides of the squaresails. When wind forces act on the front of the squaresails, the fore-and-aft strain is shifted from the backstays to the headstays, which are fewer in number and rigged only along the centerline. Backing of squaresails can be done safely in moderate winds; it is deliberately done in both tacking and boxhauling. However, the *Eagle*'s captains have found it dangerous to back her squaresails in gale force winds. Another disadvantage of tacking in rough weather is the increased difficulty of turning upwind. Heavy seas breaking against the weather bow may thwart the maneuver entirely.

One skipper's rule of thumb was this: the *Eagle* will not tack if making less than six knots; she should not tack if making 12 or more. In the first case, she would probably not go through the wind; in the latter, the true wind would be 25 knots or more, and the vessel should not be thrown aback.

There have been considerable variations from this. In smooth water, the *Eagle* has been tacked readily at speeds of less than six knots. Under rough sea conditions tacking has usually been avoided regardless of the wind force. Tacking

involves considerably more uncertainty and loss of control than wearing. These conditions are avoided when the vessel is laboring in heavy weather.

On the *Eagle,* the various sails are critical in maneuvering, each creating a specific turning effect on the ship. The headsails and foresails, being forward of the ship's pivot point, tend to turn the ship's bow away from the wind. This tendency is accentuated by the cadets' trimming the sails to present their greatest lateral area to the wind. It is minimized by their trimming the sails so that they shake or spill. The sails set on or from the mainmast, being close to the pivot point, exert little turning movement. However, they have considerable propelling power or retarding effect, depending upon whether they are drawing or backing, and this is carefully considered in all maneuvers. The spanker and mizzen staysails, being aft of the pivot point, tend to force the ship's bow up into the wind. This is accentuated by the cadets' hauling the spanker boom amidships and flattening mizzen staysail sheets. It is minimized by their taking in these staysails and hauling in the spanker.

The basic force in turning the *Eagle,* of course, is the rudder. When the cadets put the rudder hard over, there is a rapid reduction in the vessel's speed. The ship, in the initial part of the turn, is skidding sideways through the water. The greatly increased resistance encountered by the underwater body quickly reduces speed by as much as 40 per cent. This constant rudder drag acts in the manner of a large bucket hung over the stern. As the speed of the vessel drops through these forces, the turning effect of the rudder also diminishes. It is common for the *Eagle* to be dead in the water by the time she is bow-to-wind in a tacking evolution. In this case, the sails alone must continue the turn through the wind.

Because of the paramount importance of the rudder forces, the *Eagle* is usually moving at her best speed when the tacking maneuver is started. The best course has the *Eagle* sailing full-and-by, as high as possible consistent with sails drawing full. Then the wheel is turned gradually rather than suddenly. That reduces the initial slowing effect and allows angular momentum to be developed with a greater residual speed. It produces the maximum overall sustained turning effect.

Sometimes, tacking maneuvers do not work out as well as hoped, and the *Eagle* comes dead in the water when bow-to-wind, then starts backing down. Then the rudder is shifted to keep the bow swinging through the wind. If the sails are correctly handled, the vessel backs off on the new tack, then

Extra rigging comes on deck from below.

forges ahead again after the sails fill. If the sails are not properly handled or if the ship comes to a standstill before she is bow-to-wind, she falls back on the original tack. Then the cadets haul the mainyards back to the original tack, trim sail, gather speed, and try again.

Wearing is the method of bringing the *Eagle* about when weather conditions or available manpower do not permit tacking. Its advantages are that it can be accomplished by the watch on deck alone; that it does not involve backing of squaresails, and that the vessel is under full control at all times. A disadvantage is that it involves loss of distance to leeward.

The maneuver begins by putting the rudder hard over in a direction to turn the ship's bow away from the wind. At the same time, the cadets brace in the main yards until the sails are lifting. With the headsails and foresails drawing full, the mainsails lifting, and all sails on the mizzen doused, the ship's bow pays off rapidly. The main yards are braced around progressively to keep the mainsails lifting as the vessel swings downwind. As the ship approaches the downwind position, the mainsails fill and the foresails begin to go light. Then, the cadets brace around the fore yards to keep the foresails lifting. Simultaneously, the spanker is set and the headsail sheets crossed over. The ship swings rapidly upwind. When the fore yards are braced up sharp on the new tack, cadets set the mainsail, set the staysails, board the tacks, trim all sails, and square away.

When sufficient cadets are available to man both main and fore yards simultaneously, the *Eagle* can be "sailed around" through its turn at greater speed by bracing both yards progressively in such a manner as to keep all squaresails drawing to maximum advantage. This results in a more expeditious maneuver; however, it always requires more hands than the watch on deck.

Boxhauling combines certain features of tacking and wearing to permit the *Eagle* to come about with a minimum of gain or loss of distance to windward. It is used when some danger ahead precludes the headreach realized in tacking, yet the large loss of distance to leeward involved in ordinary wearing is unacceptable. The operation finds its most common application in maneuvering in a river or other narrow passageway. Boxhauling is chiefly of historical interest insofar as *Eagle* sailing is concerned.

A square-rigged vessel is "caught aback" when the wind, through accident rather than design, is blowing on the forward

Cadets use the small boats for rescue at sea—this time it's for a drill.

rather than the after sides of its squaresails. This may happen through the negligence of the helmsman who inadvertently allows the ship's bow to swing up into the wind. Or it may come about as a result of a sudden shift of wind which the cadet officer-of-the-deck had not anticipated. There is no harm in throwing the *Eagle*'s squaresails aback in moderate winds; in fact, this is deliberately done in many maneuvers. However, the rigging of the vessel is not designed to withstand very heavy strains from forward. *Eagle* officers are constantly alert to avoid this danger, particularly when the vessel is sailing close-hauled. Any momentary lapse on the part of the helmsman is immediately detected and corrected. Weather conditions are constantly studied so that sudden shifts of wind may be anticipated. If the wind becomes erratic in direction, the *Eagle* is eased off the wind until the situation clarifies.

Despite the best efforts, unforeseeable wind shifts do occur and the *Eagle,* like all other square-riggers, occasionally finds herself "caught aback."

There are several possible courses of action for recovering.

If the wind shift has been relatively minor (one to two points and has been detected immediately, the situation can usually be corrected by ordering right or left full rudder, as appropriate, and turning the ship's bow away from the wind. This type of recovery requires that the rudder be put over quickly before the backing of the squaresails has killed the ship's headway. If the ship comes dead in the water while still aback, something else is necessary.

Should the *Eagle* be unable to complete its turn away before coming dead in the water, but the wind is still on the original bow, the turn can be completed by bracing the head-yards abox and letting the spanker sheet run. This results in wind force being applied forward of the ship's pivot point, causing the bow to continue to fall off. When the mainsails begin to fill, the head yards are hauled back to the original tack and the vessel sails off.

If the wind has come around to dead ahead on the opposite bow, and there are no tactical objections to sailing on the opposite tack, recovery is made by proceeding exactly as in tacking.

The ship can also recover on the same tack by an old maneuver known as chapeling ship.

Chapeling ship is in many ways similar to boxhauling. In each maneuver, the vessel finds herself aback. In each maneuver, the vessel backs stern-to-wind the same way; then when the squaresails fill, she sails around as in wearing. The difference is that in chapeling the maneuver starts with the yards braced up on the opposite tack. Thus, the fore yards are already abox, or nearly so. As the bow pays off, the main yards are braced square and the rudder shifted to facilitate backing stern-to-wind. The ship comes around but goes into her downwind turn somewhat more slowly and completes it with more loss of distance to leeward.

When the *Eagle* is sailing full-and-by, trimmed to maximum advantage, she makes good a speed approximately half the speed of the wind. As the wind velocity increases, however, the heel of the vessel and the strain on the rigging increase accordingly.

When to start shortening sail is a matter of judgment, dependent upon the tactical situation, the state of the sea, the weather to be expected, the experience level of the cadets, the geographical location of the vessel and many other factors. There have been times when the ship has been sailed at 16 knots for sustained periods without casualty. At other times the ship has blown out sails and labored excessively at speeds of 12 knots. No fixed rules have been laid down since this is an area where a feel for the ship and an indefinable seaman's sense must control. Shortening sail unnecessarily or too early results in lost distance and failure to realize the maximum potential of the vessel. Delaying it too long can result in blown-out sails, rigging damage and possible injury to the crew.

In shortening sail, the cadets first take in the royals and topgallants, then the courses, then the upper topsails. Staysails come in from the top down. In a real blow, the men may end up with the vessel sailing under lower topsails alone or possibly hove-to under main lower topsail and fore topmast staysail. Cadet leaders and officers are always sure that the movable yards are completely in their lifts, with braces taut, before they send men out to furl. That guarantees a secure platform for the men working on the yards. They also determine that the sails are securely hauled up in their gear with buntlines, leechlines and clewlines secured on their pins. A sudden "bloomer" aloft can throw off even the hardiest of sail handlers.

When the wind force is such that furling is difficult, manpower is concentrated on the weather sides of the yardarms and the cadets furl progressively from weather to leeward, never the reverse. In rough weather, no thought is wasted on the niceties of a harbor furl; all effort is concentrated on

smothering and securing the sail as quickly and effectively as possible.

Every cadet can anticipate at least one occasion where he will be called upon to lay aloft and furl sail under conditions of darkness and high winds. This is where a "stout heart" is essential. It is actually not particularly dangerous so long as the cadets keep their heads, work with their shipmates as a team and follow a few common sense rules. *But it does take courage and determination!*

When the *Eagle* encounters a sudden sharp increase in winds, as when passing through a squall, several things are apt to happen. If the wind is anywhere forward of the quarter, the vessel increases the angle of heel. This submerges the fuller lines of the lee bow, increases the forward lateral resistance, and tends to cause the bow to fly up into the wind. Quick action on the wheel is required to avoid being caught aback. A decided lee rudder is needed to hold the vessel on its course, and this may leave little rudder in reserve for turning away and running off, should that become necessary. To ease this situation, the spanker is brailed in at the first opportunity—a tactic which markedly reduces the pressure aft of the pivot point and makes it easier to turn away.

When the ship can safely turn and run before a heavy squall, that is done. The wind velocity is reduced by the vessel's speed; the seas are following rather than ahead. The cadets can shorten sail at their leisure and with safety, then turn and continue on the desired track.

However, in heavy seas it is not always safe to turn away. There may be little residual rudder force to take the ship around, and the turn off wind can be painfully slow. During this turn the ship comes broadside to the full force of the wind. This further increases the angle of the heel and further decreases the effect of the lee rudder. The ship is then in a vulnerable position, subject to being "knocked down."

If the cadet officer-of-the-deck anticipates the squall and runs off before it hits full force, the danger is reduced. If he does not, it is often better to hold the vessel on the edge of the wind until the worst of the squall passes. That maneuver requires expert helmsmanship.

An alert cadet officer-of-the-deck will usually run off or reduce sail before the ship is struck by a heavy squall. Squalls seldom appear without warning. They are usually detected both visually and by radar well in advance of the time they envelop the ship. The problem is that most squalls do not pack dangerously high winds, and it is difficult to distinguish

those that do from those that do not. If the *Eagle* shortened sail and turned to run before every impending squall she would have trouble ever making a schedule. That is another area, therefore, where judgment and an indefinable seaman's sense prevail. When in doubt, the *Eagle*'s captain usually shortens sail or runs off before the squall hits. If the ship continues, the cadets must be ready to ride the edge of the wind and to apply a large amount of lee rudder should that become necessary. If things really get tough, and sometimes they have, a lot of wind is spilled in a hurry by throwing off the lee sheets. That action may rip some sails and foul some running rigging, but it eases the ship.

To allow the *Eagle* to ride out a heavy storm in the easiest possible manner, she is sometimes hove to. This is resorted to only when the wind and sea conditions become so adverse that the vessel can no longer safely make any distance in the desired direction. The most favorable hove-to position is with wind and sea about two points forward of the beam, with the vessel at bare steerage way. In this position the vessel may roll substantially, but she will not roll dangerously, as she might if she lay in the trough. She will take some seas over the weather bow, but she will not pound or labor as she would if she were being driven up into wind and sea.

Heaving-to with wind and sea on the quarter allows the *Eagle* to ride easily but is usually avoided because it requires close rudder control to avoid broaching. Broaching occurs when a following sea strikes the weather quarter at a time when the lee bow is submerged in a trough. This creates a turning moment which rolls the vessel to leeward and slews her around into the trough. *Under extreme conditions it is very dangerous.*

Prior to the weather's becoming so bad that the *Eagle* must heave to, lifelines are rigged, boats are secured with extra gripes and lashings, and the ship is placed in her maximum condition of watertight integrity. Likewise, stores and gear are firmly secured against shifting and banging about, free surface liquids are eliminated to the maximum extent possible, all unnecessary personnel are kept below decks, damage control gear is in maximum condition of readiness, roving security patrols are established and normal mess facilities are shut down.

The *Eagle*, when properly secured and hove to in a seamanlike manner, can survive storms of unbelievable intensity. She often has.

119

Each of the terms below was once familiar to every deep-water sailor and square-riggerman. Today they remain only in memories of old salts and among the young men who still sail the world's few remaining tall-masted training ships. On the *Eagle,* the terms noted by an asterisk are also used as commands.

ABACK—A sail is aback when the wind is striking it on the opposite side from the normal situation; done on purpose in maneuvering or can happen accidentally.

AVAST*—Cadets stop executing last command and hold what they have. They do not belay until directed.

BACKSTAY—Standing rigging leading from a point on the mast to the rail abaft the mast.

BELAY*—Cadets secure the line to the belaying pin, cleat, or other point established for the purpose.

BOARD THE TACK*—Cadets hook a special tackle (tay-kul) called the "tack jigger" in the weather clew of the foresail or mainsail and haul it down to the rail. Done when sailing closehauled.

BOBSTAY—A heavy stay (a steel rod on *Eagle*) running from the stem to the bowsprit.

BOLTROPE—Roping around the edges of a sail.

BOOM—A spar used to extend the foot of a fore and aft sail.

BOXING—A maneuver sometimes used when the *Eagle* has missed stays or has been taken aback; the head yards are kept aback and as the vessel loses headway the bow pays off rapidly to leeward, at which point, the maneuver of wearing ship may be carried through.

BRACES—Running rigging used to swing the yards in a horizontal plane.

BRACE IN—To swing the yards more athwartships or perpendicular to the keel.

BRACE UP—To swing the yards more fore and aft.

BRAILS—Lines used in furling the spanker, to bring it in to the mast.

BULL'S EYE—A round or oval wooden block without sheave. It has a groove around for the strap and a hole for the lead of a line.

BUNTLINES—Lines used to furl a squaresail and bring the foot up to the yard.

CAP—A band at the head of a mast.

CAST or CASTING—To swing the vessel's head as necessary for getting under way.

CLEAR AWAY*—A cadet lays out a coil so that the line will run freely. Applies to downhauls, weather staysail sheets, etc.

CLEW DOWN*—To haul on the clewlines while holding the sheets in order to settle a yard.

CLEW GARNETS—Special term for the clewliness of the foresail and mainsail (courses).

CLEWLINES—Lines leading to the lower corners of a squaresail to bring them up to the yardarms when furling.

CLEW UP—To bring the sail up in its gear by slacking sheets and hauling clewlines, buntlines and leechlines.

COURSES—The collective term for the foresail and mainsail. A correct usage is SET THE COURSES. Where only one mast is referred to, the words FORESAIL, MAINSAIL, FOREYARD, MAINBRACE are used. COURSES is a little used word. COURSE is reserved for the desired heading of the ship.

CRANE LINES—Athwartship cables for men to work between the shrouds—similar to ratlines.

CROSSTREES—Athwartship members located where the topmast and topgallant mast come together.

DOLPHIN STRIKER—A strut or brace extending almost vertically downward from the bowsprit to the bobstay.

DOWNHAUL—Line leading to the deck from head of a staysail for hauling it down.

EARRING—A short piece of line secured to a cringle for hauling out the head of a squaresail when bending it on the yard.

EASE*—To pay out slowly and with care; reduce strain on the line. Used for halyards, etc.

FULL AND BY—Sailing close to the wind with the sails drawing full and conforming to the changes in direction of the wind.

FURL—To take in a sail and secure it.

GAFF—A spar on the mizzen used for extending the head of the spanker.

GANTLINE—A whip (purchase) rigged aloft for general utility purposes.

GASKET—Line or canvas strap used to secure a sail when furled.

HALYARD—Running rigging used to hoist and lower sails and yards.

HAND OVER HAND*—Cadets face towards the point of pull (opposite the direction of pull) and pull first with one hand and then with the other.

HANK—Circular metal fitting which rides on a stay and to which the luff of a staysail is seized.

HEAVE AROUND*—To haul on a line by machinery. Since this is very seldom the case on the *Eagle*, the command does not deserve its present vogue. The proper command is HAUL, or one of its variations.

HEAVE TO—(UNDER SAIL) To kill the ship's headway by turning into the wind or by backing the yards on one or more masts.

INHAUL—Line used to haul in the head or foot of the spanker.

IN ITS GEAR—When a sail has been drawn up and is being held by its gear—buntlines, leechlines and clewlines.

JACKSTAY—A metal rod to which sails or lines are fastened.

JIGGER—A handy purchase (tackle), generally used to take additional strain on running rigging.

LEE—On the side away from the wind.

LEECH—The after edge of a fore-and-aft sail; the sides of a squaresail.

LEECHLINES—Lines leading to the sides of a squaresail to bring them up to the yardarms when furling.

LET GO AND HAUL*—Command to swing the yards of the foremast to the opposite tack when maneuvering under sail.

LIFTS—Standing lifts are rigged on royal, topgallant and upper topsail yards to keep them level when fully lowered; running lifts are rigged on the fore and main yards to permit canting of all the yards (with sails set) as required.

LIZARD—A short length of line having a thimble or thimbles spliced into its ends and used as a leader for rigging.

LUFF—The forward edge of a fore-and-aft sail; the shake or slat of a sail when the sheet is too slack or the vessel too close to the wind.

MAINSAIL HAUL*—Command to swing the yards of the mainmast to the opposite tack when maneuvering under sail.

MARRY—To place two lines together in order to haul them at the same time.

MASTHEAD—The top of a lower mast, where foretop or maintop is situated.

MAN*—To station sufficient men to haul on the line against the anticipated strain.

ON THE WIND—Close-hauled, or sailing as close to the wind as possible.

OUTHAUL—Line used to haul out the head or the foot of the spanker.

OVERHAUL*—Command to assist in rendering freely. Applies to extending a tackle, pulling up slack in buntlines, etc.

PEAK—The upper after corner of a fore-and-aft sail.

PENDANT—A short piece of line or wire with an eye at each end used for hanging off a block, footrope, etc.

POLE—The upper end of the highest mast, between the royal yard and the truck.

RISE TACKS AND SHEETS*—Command to clew up the mainsail when maneuvering under sail.

ROBAND—Short length of marlin used to secure the head of a squaresail to the jackstay, or the luff of a headsail to the hanks.

ROUND IN*—To bring the blocks of a tackle together by hauling on the line.

RUN AWAY WITH*—Cadets face in the direction of pull, grasp the line with both hands and run.

RUNNING RIGGING—Moveable lines and blocks used for controlling sails, yards, etc.

SHEET—Running rigging secured to the clew of a sail (opposing a clewline).

SHROUDS—Standing rigging used to support a mast laterally, led athwartships from aloft to the rail.

SLACK*—Command to pay out fairly rapidly; to remove most of the strain from the line.

SPREADER—Extension projecting horizontally at the crosstrees to spread backstays.

STANDING PART—The fixed part of any piece of running rigging; the end which is secured permanently.

STAYS—Standing rigging in line with the ship's keel; some stays carry staysails. A vessel "in stays" has the wind fore-and-aft sail.

TACK—A line leading forward from the clew of the foresail or mainsail; the lower forward corner of a fore-and-aft sail.

TACKING—A sailing maneuver; the process of bringing the ship's head through the wind to get the wind on the opposite side.

TACK JIGGER—A tackle used to haul down the weather tack of a foresail or mainsail.

TEND*—To station one cadet or at most two for the purpose of slacking or keeping the slack out of a line.

THAT'S WELL*—Basically same meaning as AVAST. Used in final trimming. For example: HAUL ON YOUR WEATHER (FORE) BRACES—THAT'S WELL THE FOREBRACE, WELL THE UPPER TOPSAIL BRACE, WELL THE ROYAL BRACE, WELL ALL BELAY.

THROAT—The forward upper corner of a fore-and-aft sail.

THROW OFF*—To take a line off pin and see that it runs freely. Never applies to lines under a heavy load, i.e., halyards, except in real emergencies. Used for buntlines when setting sail.

TIMENOGUY—A line stretched from one point to another for the purpose of preventing gear from fouling; a piece of light line with a bull's eye spliced in the end. It serves to support long and heavy line like the main brace which passes through the bull's eye.

TOP—Platform at the top of a mast, as foretop or maintop, not the actual uppermost point.

TOPPING LIFT—Purchase used for raising or taking the weight off a boom.

TRIM*—Implies an adjustment of a sail by hauling in on sheet (fore-and-aft sails) or brace.

UNFURL—To cast loose a sail by throwing off the gaskets.

VANG—A line leading from the mizzen gaff to the deck to keep it steady when the spanker is not set (used in pairs on *Eagle*).

WEATHER—On the side toward the wind.

WEARING—A sailing maneuver; the process of bringing the ship's stern through the wind to get the wind on the opposite side.

YARD—A spar rigged horizontally on a mast, to which the head of a squaresail is bent (made fast).

Appendix B: Eagle Sailing Orders

When ordered to sailing stations aboard the *Eagle,* cadets can expect to hear any of these commands from the cadet officer-of-the-deck echoed by the mast captains. Each command brings a dozen or more men into action during a sailing maneuver.

To set a lower topsail:
YARDMEN LAY LOFT AND LOOSE THE FORE (MAIN) LOWER TOPSAIL. MAN THE FORE (MAIN) LOWER TOPSAIL SHEETS. LET FALL, LAY IN AND OVERHAUL GEAR. THROW OFF THE BUNTLINES, EASE THE CLEWLINES. SHEET HOME AND BELAY.

To set an upper topsail:
YARDMAN LAY ALOFT AND LOOSE THE FORE (MAIN) UPPER TOPSAIL. MAN THE FORE (MAIN) UPPER TOPSAIL SHEETS AND HALYARD. TEND THE LEE BRACE; LET FALL, LAY IN AND OVERHAUL GEAR, THROW OFF THE BUNTLINES. EASE THE CLEWLINES, THROW OFF THE TOPGALLANT SHEETS, SHEET HOME AND BELAY. WALK AWAY (THEN HAND OVER HAND) WITH THE UPPER TOPSAIL HALYARD, EASE THE LEE BRACE.

To set a topgallant sail:
YARDMEN LAY ALOFT AND LOOSE THE FORE (MAIN) T'GANTSAIL, MAN THE FORE (MAIN) T'GANTSAIL SHEETS AND HALYARD. TEND THE LEE BRACE, LET FALL, LAY IN AND OVERHAUL GEAR, THROW OFF THE BUNTLINES, EASE THE CLEWLINES, THROW OFF THE ROYAL SHEETS, SHEET HOME AND BELAY. WALK AWAY (THEN HAND OVER HAND) WITH THE T'GALLANT HALYARD. EASE THE LEE BRACE.

To set a royal sail:
YARDMAN LAY ALOFT AND LOOSE THE FORE (MAIN) ROYAL, MAN THE FORE (MAIN) SHEETS AND HALYARD. TEND THE LEE BRACE, LET FALL, LAY IN AND OVERHAUL GEAR. THROW OFF THE BUNTLINES, EASE THE CLEWLINES, SHEET HOME AND BELAY. WALK AWAY (THEN HAND OVER HAND) WITH THE ROYAL HALYARD. EASE THE LEE BRACE.

To set courses (braced up):
YARDMAN LAY ALOFT AND LOOSE THE FORESAIL (MAINSAIL), MAN THE FORE (MAIN) WEATHER TACK AND LEE SHEET, TEND THE LEE TACK AND WEATHER SHEET, LET FALL, LAY IN AND OVERHAUL GEAR. THROW OFF THE BUNTLINES AND LEECHLINES, EASE THE CLEWGARNETS, EASE THE WEATHER LIFT AND BOARD THE TACK, HAUL AFT THE LEE SHEET (When not braced up both sheets are manned then let fall and sheeted home.).

To set the spanker:
INSURE THAT THE RADIO TRANSMITTERS ARE SECURED BEFORE SENDING MEN ALOFT. TEND THE SPANKER SHEET, RIG THE PREVENTER. HAUL THE SPANKER BOOM TO PORT (STARBOARD).

SLACK THE WEATHER VANG. TOP THE BOOM. LAY ALOFT AND CLEAR AWAY THE SPANKER.

When the sail is loosed:
LAY IN AND OVERHAUL THE BRAILS, SLACK THE INHAULS, SLACK THE BRAILS, HAUL AWAY ON THE OUTHAULS (It is necessary here to avoid fouling the colors.).

If necessary, after the sail is set:
EASE THE TOPPING LIFT, ROUND IN THE SLACK IN THE VANGS.

To set the gaff topsail:
INSURE THAT THE RADIO TRANSMITTERS ARE SECURED BEFORE SENDING MEN ALOFT. LAY ALOFT AND CLEAR AWAY THE GAFF TOPSAIL, MAN THE GAFF TOPSAIL SHEET AND HALYARD, TEND THE GAFF TOPSAIL CLEWLINE, SLACK THE CLEWLINES, LAUL AWAY ON THE HALYARD, SHEET HOME. SECURE THE TACK.

To set a staysail or headsail:
LAY OUT (OR ALOFT) AND CLEAR AWAY THE _____, MAN THE _____ HALYARD, CLEAR AWAY AND TEND THE DOWNHAUL, TEND THE SHEET(S), WALK AWAY WITH THE _____ HALYARD (Hand over hand the last few feet), SHEET HOME.

To take in a royal:
MAN THE FORE (MAIN) ROYAL CLEWLINES AND BUNTLINES; TEND THE SHEETS, HALYARD AND LEE BRACE. EASE THE HALYARD, CLEW DOWN, ROUND IN THE LEE BRACE. When the yard is in the lifts, CLEW UP (The sheets are thrown off and the buntlines hauled in addition to the clewlines.) BELAY.

To take in a topgallant sail:
MAN THE FORE (MAIN) TOPGALLANT CLEWLINESS AND BUNTLINES; TEND THE SHEETS, HALYARDS, AND LEE BRACE. THROW OFF THE ROYAL SHEETS, EASE THE HALYARD, CLEW DOWN, ROUND IN THE LEE BRACE. When the yard is in the lift, CLEW UP (The sheets are thrown off and the buntlines hauled in addition to the clewlines.) BELAY.

To take in an upper topsail:
MAN THE FORE (MAIN) UPPER TOPSAIL BUNTLINES AND CLEWLINES; TEND THE SHEETS, HALYARD, AND LEE BRACE. THROW OFF THE TOPGALLANT SHEETS, EASE THE HALYARD, CLEW DOWN, ROUND IN THE LEE BRACE. When the yard is in the lifts, CLEW UP (The sheets are thrown off and the buntlines hauled in addition to the clewlines.) BELAY.

To take in courses:
MAN THE FORE (MAIN) CLEW GARNETS, BUNTLINES AND LEECHLINES. TEND THE TACKS AND SHEETS, SET TAUT BOTH LIFTS AND BELAY. CLEAR AWAY THE TACK JIGGER, SLACK TACKS AND SHEETS, CLEW UP (The alternative command "Rise tacks and sheets" may be used.) BELAY.

To take in the lower topsail:
MAIN THE FORE (MAIN) LOWER TOPSAIL CLEWLINES AND BUNTLINES, THROW OFF THE SHEETS AND CLEW UP, BELAY.

To take in a jib or staysail:
LEAD OUT AND MAN THE _____ DOWNHAUL, CLEAR AWAY THE _____ HALYARD, TEND THE SHEET, SLACK THE _____ HALYARD, WALK AWAY WITH THE _____ DOWNHAUL (The sheet is eased as the hanks bind on the stay.).

To take in the spanker:
TOP THE SPANKER BOOM, LEAD OUT AND TEND THE OUTHAULS, MAN THE BRAILS AND INHAULS, THROW OFF THE OUTHAULS, HAUL DOWN, BRAIL IN (If the wind has been free and the boom eased to the point where the sail would bind against the lee rigging when taken in, the preventer is eased and the boom hauled more inboard.).

To take in the gaff topsail:
MAN THE GAFF TOPSAIL CLEWLINE, TEND THE SHEET AND HALYARD, THROW OFF THE TACK, SLACK THE SHEET AND HALYARD, HAUL DOWN.

Pictorial Contributors

ROBERT de GAST, a native of Holland, is a free-lance photographer who has contributed more pictures to the U.S. Naval Institute than any other photographer. He has an in-born interest in the sea and in ships of all types. His photographs of the *Eagle* represent the finest black-and-white shots of this ship in existence. Pp. 29, 30, 33, 36, 37, 40, 41, 44, 45, 49, 53, 56-57, 60, 64, 69, 73, 80, 81, 85, 88, 93, 96, 97, 109 and 117.

EASTMAN KODAK COMPANY, PHOTOGRAPHIC ILLUSTRATIONS DIVISION is part of the corporate organization of this world-famous manufacturer of photographic equipment and film. Pp. 46-47, 50, 54, 58, 59, 63, 74-75, 106.

JOHN E. FLETCHER is a staff photographer for the National Geographic Society. He has extensive work in *National Geographic* magazine on a variety of subjects. His photography also includes some of the most dramatic illustrations of life aboard the *Eagle*. Pp. 86-87 and 98-99. Copyright © National Geographic Society.

A. B. HOW is a captain in the United States Coast Guard and an amateur photographer. He is a graduate of the Coast Guard Academy, Class of 1947, and has served as as officer aboard five Coast Guard cutters including the *Campbell* and the *Westwind*. Captain How has commanded the Cutters *Jonquil* and *Mariposa*. While assigned to the Academy as head of the Seamanship Section and the Department of Humanities, Captain How was skipper of the *Eagle* for three years. Pp. 38 and 83.

NATIONAL BROADCASTING COMPANY, SPECIAL PROJECTS DIVISION, is responsible for the *Project 21* television special presentation, "Down to the Sea in Ships." This hour-long color production is a romantic recounting of men, the sea and their use of ships. Pp. 6 and 10. Copyright © National Broadcasting Company.

WILLIAM I. NORTON is the author of this book and editor of a previous work, *Eagle Seamanship; Square Rigger Sailing,* currently used as a manual for sailing the *Eagle* by the cadets of the Coast Guard Academy. Pp. 34 and 35.

DAVID A. SANDELL, a lieutenant commander in the United States Coast Guard, is a graduate of the Coast Guard Academy, Class of 1961. He is an amateur photographer who photographed the *Eagle* both during cruises as a cadet, and later, as a Seamanship instructor and Commandant-of-Cadets. Mr. Sandell has been an officer aboard the Coast Guard Cutters *Eastwind,* which sailed to the Antarctic, and *Hawthorn*. After completing His Master of Science Degree, he taught Mathematics at the Academy. P. 102.

GEORGE SILK is a staff photographer for and frequent contributor to *Life* magazine. A series of articles devoted to the United States Coast Guard and beautifully illustrated by Mr. Silk recently appeared in *Life*. Pp. 18-19, 39, 67, 70, 95, 111, 114 and back cover.

ROBERT F. SISSON is a staff photographer for the National Geographic Society. With a special love of the sea, Mr. Sisson has often contributed to articles on maritime lore in *National Geographic* magazine. He also contributed to the Society's book, *Men, Ships and the Sea*. P. 118. Copyright © National Geographic Society.

UNITED STATES COAST GUARD ACADEMY, PUBLIC INFORMATION OFFICE is the official public relations and information arm for the Coast Guard Academy. Its Photographic Section has an extensive collection of *Eagle* photography. Pp. 13, 35, 42, 51, 79, 91, 113 and 115.

UNITED STATES COAST GUARD, OFFICE OF PUBLIC AND INTERNATIONAL AFFAIRS acts as the official spokesman for the Coast Guard in all matters. Its Public Information Division maintain files of thousands of color and black-and-white photographs of Coast Guard activities and subjects. Among those well-documented is the *Eagle*. Pp. 31, 43, 55 and 77.

ALAN VILLIERS has to his credit a long line of distinguished books on the great days of sail, including *Sailing Eagle* and *Men, Ships and the Sea.* He went to sea from his native Australia at the age of 15 and has been there in one way or another ever since. At one point, he was owner and captain of the former whaler *Joseph Conrad,* sailing her over the seas as a school ship. Today, he makes his home in Oxford, England, where he continues to recount the lore of seafaring. P. 90. Copyright © National Geographic Society.

Index